TWAYNE'S WORLD AUTHORS SERIES

A Survey of the World's Literature

Sylvia E. Bowman, Indiana University

GENERAL EDITOR

CHINA

William R. Schultz, University of Arizona

EDITOR

The Book of Songs

(TWAS 177)

TWAYNE'S WORLD AUTHORS SERIES (TWAS)

The purpose of TWAS is to survey the major writers —novelists, dramatists, historians, poets, philosophers, and critics—of the nations of the world. Among the national literatures covered are those of Australia, Canada, China, Eastern Europe, France, Germany, Greece, India, Italy, Japan, Latin America, New Zealand, Poland, Russia, Scandinavia, Spain, and the African nations, as well as Hebrew, Yiddish, and Latin Classical literatures. This survey is complemented by Twayne's United States Authors Series and English Authors Series.

The intent of each volume in these series is to present a critical-analytical study of the works of the writer; to include biographical and historical material that may be necessary for understanding, appreciation, and critical appraisal of the writer and to present all material in clear, concise English—but not to vitiate the scholarly content of the work by doing so.

The Book of Songs

By WILLIAM McNAUGHTON
Oberlin College

Twayne Publishers, Inc.   ::   New York

For my Mother
tertius mittitur hic tibi libellus

Preface

Some translators have called it, after its first part, *The Book of Songs*; some have called it, after its third part, *The Book of Odes*. The Chinese themselves call it *Shih Ching*: "The Poetry Classic." Classic it has been, from the time of Confucius (551-479 B.C.). When the new government of the Republic of China wanted a national anthem, they composed it in a *Book of Songs* meter.

Why has this book of poems meant so much to the Chinese? Why has it lasted so long? What influence has it had on Chinese literature, on Chinese civilization, during the twenty-five hundred years of its existence? Such are the questions I asked before I wrote this study. I don't claim that my reader will find "the answers" to them, but I have tried, in comparatively brief space, to bring him closer to the three hundred and five poems themselves, where the answers must lie.

Great progress during the last hundred years has been made in Sinological studies. Of the progress that has been linguistic and philological, I have made a great deal of use. But modern studies that attempt to show "the true meaning of the Classics" —whether by Marcel Granet or Kuo Mo-jo or Timothy Leary— I have treated as less important than what the Chinese reader himself, for twenty-five hundred years, thought to be their true meaning. W. A. C. H. Dobson had warned me against "bright French guesses."

The book is divided into two parts, one called "Subjects," one called "Style."

The section on "Subjects" deals with the most important basic Chinese ideas that receive expression in *The Book of Songs*: *li* (rites), *jen* (*humanitas*), *i* (equity), *chih* (learning), *te* (personal virtue, or energy), *tao* (Tao), and *wu-wei* (anti-action). I talk in several chapters (namely, 3, 4, 5, 6, 7) about such subjects as war, separation, love, idleness, and such themes as *carpe diem* —subjects which may be more familiar to the Western reader as subjects of poetry.

Style in *The Book of Songs* is important to any student of Chinese poetry, if for no other reason than the fact that the

Songs contain the original stock of Chinese poetic expression. In my treatment of style, I make much use of contemporary Chinese scholarship. I believe that the reader will find described in some new detail the actual elements of poetic expression in Chinese. Wang Li in *Chinese Poetics,* for example, talks about seven rhetorical figures; in the present book thirty-four rhetorical figures are discussed. The only other book in English on this subject discusses three. I have tried in every case to show how the poet uses form to serve content or uses the form so that it becomes part of the content.

About Chinese language and literature, I learned a great deal from Tien-yi Li, Hans Frankel, Hugh Stimson, Chou Fa-kao, Imataka Makoto, and Ogawa Tamaki. About poetry and poetic expression, I learned much from Ezra Pound, Al Fineman, and Lenore Mayhew. Thomas Bergin, *cortese e ardito,* translator and poet, allowed me to audit his course at Yale in Provençal poetry, and his course in Dante. The editors of *The Journal of the American Oriental Society* have allowed me to reprint in Chapter 12 part of an article I published in that journal. I did some of the work which went into this study as part of my doctoral dissertation at Yale, "Shih Ching Rhetoric: Schemes of Words," and I am indebted to all those who helped me do the earlier study. For permissions to quote, I am indebted to Lenore Mayhew, to Charles E. Tuttle Co., to Harcourt Brace, to New Directions, to Far Eastern Publications (Yale University), and to Cambridge University Press. I am especially indebted to Harvard University Press for permission to quote generously from Pound's translation of *The Book of Songs.*

The dedication is to my mother, who gave me a lute when I needed it. "Barring cogent reasons," Confucius says, "a scholar is never without his lute."

Contents

Acknowledgments

Material from *The Classic Anthology* reprinted by permission of the publishers from Ezra Pound, trans., *The Classic Anthology Defined by Confucius*, Cambridge, Mass.: Harvard University Press, Copyright 1954 by the President and Fellows of Harvard College; from William Carlos Williams, *Collected Earlier Poems*, Copyright 1938 by William Carlos Williams, reprinted by permission of New Directions Publishing Corporation, and of MacGibbon and Kee, Ltd., publishers for the British Commonwealth except Canada; from E. E. Cummings, *Poems 1923-1954*, Copyright, 1926, by Horace Liveright; renewed, 1954, by E. E. Cummings, by permission of Harcourt Brace Jovanovich, Inc.

Chronology

(All dates are B.C.)

1765	Shang Dynasty founded.
after 1719	Poems 301, 302, 304 composed.
after 1264	Poems 303, 305 composed.
1185-1135	The Elegant King (Wen-2).
1122	Battle at Mu Plain. The Martial King (Wu-3) defeats the Shang; founds the Chou dynasty (cf. nos. 236 and 300).
after 1121	Poems 1-25 composed. Duke of Chou composes poems 161-63, 165-70, 237-42.
1115	The Perfect King (Ch'eng-2) ascends the throne. He is assisted in his rule by the duke of Chou, acting as regent.
after 1115	Duke of Chou composes poems 154-56, 164, 171-76, 235-36, 243-52, 266-96. Poems 157-60 composed.
1104	Duke of Chou dies.
934-909	The Virtuous King (I-4). Poems 96-100 composed.
894-878	The Peaceful King (I-2). Poem 26 composed.
878-828	The Stern King (Li-4). Poems 136-37, 146-49 (which may belong rather to the reign of the Peaceful King), 193-96, 253-57 composed.
841-827	Period of "Joint Rule" by the dukes of Chou and Shao (not, of course, the same duke of Chou as died in 1104). Poem 114 composed.
827-781	The Comprehensive King (Hsuan-1). Poems 45, 126, 138-40, 177-90, 258-63 composed.
781-770	The Dark King (Yu-1). Poems 191-92, 197-234, 264-65 composed.
771	Barbarians and rebels destroy Hao, the Chou capital, and the dynasty's real power is extinguished. Capital re-established at Lo-yang, and the "Eastern Chou Period" begins (ends 256 B.C.).
770-719	The Tranquil King (P'ing-2). Poems 27, 55-57, 65-69, 71, 75-78, 80-82, 115-21, 127-30 composed.
722	Duke Yin assumes the rule of Lu: "Spring and Autumn Period" begins (ends 481 B.C.).

719-696	The Soldierly King (Huan-2). Poems 28-44, 46-49, 58-60, 62-63, 70, 72-73, 83, 87, 107-13 (which may belong to the time of the Tranquil King), 141 composed.
696-681	The Serene King (Chuang-1). Poems 74, 84-86, 88-92, 101-6 composed.
681-676	The Correct King (Li-2). Poems 93-95, 122-23 composed.
676-651	The Kind King (Hui-4). Poems 50-54, 64, 79, 124-25, 142-43, 150 composed.
651-618	The Helpful King (Hsiang-1). Poems 61, 131-35, 151-53, 297-300 composed.
606-585	The Certain King (Ting-4). Poems 144-45 composed.
570	Lao-tzu born.
551	Confucius born.
518-511	Sometime during these eight years, Confucius meets Lao-tzu and asks him about *li*.
484	Confucius returns from Wei to Lu and brings with him songs gathered on his travels.
484-479	Confucius does his main (?) work on *The Book of Songs*.
481	"Spring and Autumn Period" ends.
479	Confucius dies.
403	"Warring States Period" begins.
255	Ch'in dynasty founded.
221	In the twenty-sixth year of his reign, the Administrative King (Cheng-4) declares himself "First Emperor"; "Warring States Period" ends.
213	Books burned at behest of the "First Emperor."
206	Ch'in dynasty extinguished; Han dynasty founded.
191	Han dynasty rescinds Ch'in's ban on the classics.
191-129	Various texts of *The Book of Songs* circulate.
129	The Gift-giving king of Ho-chien presents Mao Ch'ang's text of *The Book of Songs* to the Han court. Soon Mao's text becomes the standard text.

PART 1

Subjects

CHAPTER 1

"The Confucian Anthology"

CHINESE civilization was based on five books, and the most important of the five probably was a book of poetry—*The Book of Songs*.[1] Confucius in his conversations talks a lot about it, and some people believe that Confucian philosophy rests solidly on *The Book of Songs*. With good reason, it has been called "The Confucian Anthology."

I *Organization of* The Book of Songs

The Book of Songs contains three hundred and five songs, which are divided into three major sections: (1) "Airs of the States," 160 songs; (2) "Courtly Songs," 105 songs; and (3) "Odes," 40 songs.

The "Airs of the States" present the folk and their life. The "Courtly Songs" present the rulers and their life. The "Odes" present religious beliefs. Although one may find a few poems that do not seem to fit into this scheme, the pattern in general holds good. No one ever mentions the beauty of this over-all design, which is one of the most exciting things about the songs. Scholars often say that "the Chinese have no epic."

Goethe, I think, was the first modern man to have a vision of *Weltliteratur*. But whoever put together *The Book of Songs* had some similar vision, at least of the civilized world as he saw it. The "Airs of the States" are folk songs collected from the various localities which were then at the center as well as on the peripheries of Chinese culture. Because of the rhymes and of the linguistic uniformity, we can assume that songs in nonstandard dialect were revised so as to be both intelligible and artistically pleasing to one specific public. The first 160 *Songs*, then, were an early Chinese version of the UNESCO "International Translation Series."

The 105 "Courtly Songs" include 74 "Minor Courtly Songs" and 31 "Major Courtly Songs." Chu Hsi says that the "Minor

Courtly Songs" were sung at festal entertainments at the court and that the "Major Courtly Songs" were sung at gatherings of the feudal princes.

The "Odes" are also called "Odes of the Temple and Altar." The "Great Preface" says of them, "The 'Odes' describe perfect virtue in its beauty, so as to announce its attainment to the Spiritual and Radiant Beings."

II Collection of The Songs

Later on in China, the imperial government collected folk songs—"street-corner and narrow alley songs"—from the various localities. The government wanted to know what the people were up to, and it wanted to check on the local governor: it used the people's songs to do these things. During the Han dynasty (206 B.C.—A.D. 220), the government set up an office—the Yüeh-fu, or Music Bureau—to collect songs. The bureau collected the songs, evaluated them, and preserved them. It is due to the Music Bureau and its workings, that we have still so much of early Chinese nonscholarly poetry.[2]

The lore is, *The Book of Songs* was collected in this same way. Ssu-ma Ch'ien (145—after 86 B.C.) wrote it down as historical fact that three thousand songs, thus collected, existed in Confucius's time. Confucius picked from these three thousand songs the three hundred and five songs in *The Songs,* plus six other songs which later were lost.[3] Skepticism, however, is the faith of our age, so we no longer believe that Confucius had anything significant to do in the preparation of the anthology. Modern scholarship allows that he may have edited the music for a few songs or set type for an early edition. What is important to us, in considering *The Songs* as ancient *Weltliteratur,* is the scope and coherence of the collection. When evaluating the position of *The Songs* in Chinese literature as a whole, the fact that for twenty-one hundred years the Chinese believed Confucius to have selected them is an important consideration.

III The Songs *and Chinese Empire*

To understand how important *The Book of Songs* has been in China, we must appreciate that diverse and even antagonistic regions and regional subcultures make up China.

In China in 600 B.C., one bandit gang fought with another for major privileges and prerogatives. The people—including, in at least one case, Confucius and his students—tried to get out of the way of the armies. Nobody paid much attention to the Chou rulers, who were supposed to be "emperors of all China." Three hundred years later, in Mencius's time, things were not much better. Mencius said, "The man who unifies China, will be a man who abhors bloodshed." Historians and students have sneered at him for two millennia for that remark.

Some people say it is Confucianism that at times holds China's various regions and subcultures together to form the Chinese nation, and some people say it is ancestor worship—which may come to the same thing. Some people say it is the written language that holds them together.[4] Whichever of these, or whatever part of them, is right, *The Book of Songs* has played a most important role. I am not going to suggest that *The Songs produce* any cohesive force. Confucius said, "If decent men govern for three generations, we could get rid of the death penalty"; but we know that he did not really edit *The Songs* and that Mencius was an idealistic fool.

IV *Confucian Values*

One reason the Chinese people have respected Confucius for millennia is that Confucius respected Chinese popular values. Confucius was less than any major philosopher a "founder" or "revelator." It is what led Voltaire to say, "I admire Confucius. He was the first teacher not to receive divine illumination." Confucius himself admitted it. "I'm a transmitter," he said, "not an inventor." What he transmitted was the values which the Chinese people for ages before him had cherished. So it's not so much that China is Confucian, as that Confucianism is Chinese. The best way for us to arrive at a knowledge of Confucianism, and of how Confucian values inform *The Songs,* is to note the values as they appear in songs we read.

V The Songs *as Poetry*

Besides being a repository of Confucian values, *The Songs* are "pure poetry" in that they present us an image, more rather than less full, of the people that wrote and sang them and of the period in which they were written and sung. We can, as Confucius said, learn from *The Songs* "the names of many birds, beasts, bugs, and fish." We can learn a good deal about Chinese material civilization of that time—the musical instruments they played, the artifacts they used and enjoyed, the clothes they wore. We can learn something of the "official" or "textbook" history of the period—the rulers they feared, the battles they fought, the victories they remembered, the victories they forgot.

But most of all, we can enjoy from *The Songs* an experience of what it was like to be inside a Chinese skin in those days. For the authors speak to us in *The Songs,* loud and clear, about what they love and what they deride, of what delights them and of what annoys them. Next to sitting down with a man for coffee and conversation, hearing his poems is perhaps the best way to find out what is on his mind.

As to the man of ancient China, "what is on his mind" isn't always orthodox Confucian thought, and what stirs his soul isn't always orthodox Confucian sentiment. The songs in Chapter 7 on "Tao" express Taoist attitudes or reveal a Taoist vision (the philosophers divide Chinese thought for us into "Confucianism versus Taoism"). The Chinese themselves rather feel that every Chinese has in him a dual soul, half-Confucian, half-Taoist. It is the Taoist half that puts itself into the "Tao" songs. Confucius himself, in fact, had misgivings about some of the songs that got into the anthology. He says, "Banish the songs of Cheng!"[5]

CHAPTER 2

The Social Order

CONFUCIUS is more interested in "the necessities of government, and of governmental administration than any other philosopher."[1] Of his basic ideas about government and governmental administration, none is more important than the doctrine of *cheng ming*, or "calling things by the right name." We look at *cheng ming* later on when we study style, which seems more appropriate.[2] Laying *cheng ming* aside, then, we will in this chapter look at the basic Confucian ideas about social order, government, and governmental administration, as they are found in *The Book of Songs*.

I *"Heaven's Mandate"*

The first thing to understand about Chinese ideas on government is the concept of *T'ien-ming*, or "Heaven's mandate," which amounts to a theory of justified revolution. Simply put: the imperial family gets the rule by heavenly dispensation; by heavenly dispensation, the emperor gets his role as co-ordinator of earthly, human, and divine. The important point is in *The Book of Documents*: "Heaven's mandate is not given in perpetuity."[3]

For the rulers, then, the all-important question became: how does one retain the mandate? Two theories prevailed: (1) it was a question of luck, charisma, or something which, when the king had it, the tribe or nation shared in it, and when the king lost it, signs and portents warned of an impending calamity; (2) it was a question of governing well, so that the people flourished and prospered, and when the kings ceased to govern well, "human signs" like poverty, riots, conspiracies, and assassinations showed that the mandate would be taken away and given to others. The Confucians believed the latter theory. It was Mencius who gave the most dramatic voice to this theory. Asked if his subjects had not done wrong to rise and assassinate

17

King Chou, Mencius said, "I didn't hear that any 'King Chou' was assassinated. I did hear that the people killed a burglar by that name." (It may take the theory of *cheng ming* fully to clarify the anecdote.)

When the king *did* have the mandate (for whatever reason), the people lived happily and well, and even the state's birds, beasts, and fish benefited from the perfect co-ordination of earthly, human, and divine forces. According to *The Book of Documents*, I Yin (eighteenth century B.C.) said, "The earlier [*sic*] sovereigns . . . cultivated earnestly their virtue, and . . . the spirits of the hills and rivers likewise were all in tranquility, the birds and beasts, the fishes and tortoises, all realized the happiness of their nature." The song "Fish in Tsao" expresses this idea and connects it to "the Mandate of Heaven" (no. 221):[4]

Fish in Tsao

Fine fish in weed, that is their place.
And the king's good wine in his palace.

Fish in pond-weed wagging a tail
And the king in high Hao at his wassail.

While fish in pond-weed lie at ease
The kings of Hao may live as they please.

II "Tê": *Personal Virtue*

It will help us understand the total picture, at this point, if we understand the stress the Confucians laid on *tê*. We can translate *tê* as "personal virtue," although maybe we should knock the "e" off it and save the manhood, as in *vir, virtu. Tê* definitely contains the idea of personal energy and force. "You carry on the government," said Confucius, "The proper man's personal virtue [*tê*] is wind, the inferior man's personal virtue is grass. Grass with wind above it must bend." Disorder spreads from the center outward (or from the top downward, if you like), and good order grows from the center outward. The song "The Wicker is Broke" rebukes the Lady of Ts'i for not keeping her attendants and entourage in order, and this disorder in her retinue is supposed to proceed from defects in her own character. "Loose fish" is a term for immorals (no. 104).

The Wicker is Broke

The wicker of the weir is broke,
loose fish are out again
as the Lady of Ts'i comes home
with a cloud in her train.

The wicker of the weir is broke
as ex-Miss Ts'i comes home again,
luce and perch be broken out
as many as drops of rain.

The wicker of the weir is broke
and these fish make a very great clatter.
The Lady of Ts'i comes home with a train,
all of them loose as water.

When the ruler invests his energy as he ought, the people will
be able *and willing* 'to apply themselves with all their energy"
(*Documents,* IV, V, VI, 11). *The Book of Songs* records how
the people came *because they wanted* to build King Wen's
"Spirit Tower" (poem no. 242):

The Spirit Tower

When he planned to begin a spirit tower
folk rushed to the work-camp and overran
all the leisure of King Wen's plan;
old and young with never a call
had it up in no time at all.

The king stood in his "Park Divine,"
deer and doe lay there so fine,
so fine so sleek; birds of the air
flashed a white wing while fishes splashed
on wing-like fin in the haunted pool.

Great drums and gongs
hung on spiked frames
sounding to perfect rule and rote
about the king's calm crescent moat,

Tone unto tone, of drum and gong.

About the king's calm crescent moat
the blind musicians beat lizard skin
as the tune weaves out and in.

III   *The "One-Man" Principle*

Another important point in Confucian theory is the idea that "it may depend on one man." Now this often is taken to mean "*the* one man, that is, the emperor." And to be sure, the "one man" may often be that one man. But there is ample evidence in the Confucian classics that the principle should not be limited to the emperor alone.

The *Analects* says:

One day, some guy said to Confucius, "Maestro, why do you not hold office in the government?" Confucius replied, "What does the *Book of Documents* say about filiality? It says that even just being filial and friendly with your brothers, elder and younger, you may extend your influence to those that hold the governmental power. This also is to 'hold office.' Why do you consider that they only 'hold an office' who sit in it?" (II, 21)[5]

IV   *"The Four Foundations"*

A third important point in this theory of government is that *tê* (personal virtue) rests on four bases: humanitas (*jen*), education (*chih*), equity (*i*), and ritual and manners (*li*).

Jen: Humanitas. Of *jen* (*humanitas*), the *Book of Documents* says, "The ruler should feel the people's sufferings as his own." *The Book of Documents* also records that the Duke of Chou said, "the superior man . . . understands the hardships of sowing and reaping . . . and so he understands what it involves for the ordinary man to survive."

The duke of Chou wrote song 156 in gratitude to the people, how hard they had worked for his house and its dynastic rule. The people wrote an answering poem, "Axes Broken" (no. 157), to show that they knew he knew of their sufferings and hardship and to say that they appreciated it that he appreciated them.

Axes Broken

Axes broken, hatchets lacking,
Eastward packing, the Duke of Chou gained
four states, and the Emperor reigned
over them all. He pitied our men,
Yet they were trained.

> We have blunted our axes,
> We lack work-tools,
> Chou's Duke invades and rules as is fit
> the four states of the East to their benefit;
> Pity our men's condition,
> his praise carries them on.
>
> Axes broken, work-tools lacking,
> Chou's duke corrected
> four states and connected
> them all under one rule and test;
> By his pity of fighting men
> they now find rest.

Tax is an area where a government especially can show its benevolence, or otherwise. The *Mencius* begins with a conversation in which a ruler asks Mencius what he knows that will profit the state, and Mencius replies, "Why must your majesty use that word profit?"

We find in the songs many complaints against high taxes. "Rats" is one of the best of them (no. 113):

Rats

> RATS,
> stone-head rats lay off our grain
> three years pain,
> enough, enough, plus enough again.
> More than enough from you, deaf you,
> we're about thru and ready to go
> where something will grow
> untaxed.
> Good earth, good sown,
> and come into our own.
>
> RATS,
> big rats, lay off our wheat,
> three years deceit,
> and now we're about ready to go
> to Lo Kuo, happy, happy land, Lo Kuo, good earth
> where we can earn our worth.
>
> RATS,
> stone-head rats, spare our new shoots,
> three years, no pay.

> We're about ready to move away
> to some decent border town.
> Good earth, good sown,
> and make an end to this endless moan.

The final area to which we may look for evidence of the government's benevolence, or *humanitas*, is *law*—the way its laws are framed and executed. The law is not discussed in the *Songs* in any technical or detailed way; we only find praise for those who administer it well and blame for those who administer it ill. But it will not hurt our understanding of the praise given and the blame directed if we understand what *The Book of Documents* says about rule and law. Of law, *The Book of Documents* says "1) Do not use laws as a means of oppression; 2) When there are doubts as to the infliction of any of the five punishments, that infliction should be forborne. 3) Gain not by the decision of cases. Gain by the decision of cases is no precious acquisition: it is an accumulation of guilt, and will be recompensed with many evils." The last point, with regard to the acceptance of bribes by judges, has been of utmost interest to the Chinese throughout their history. The Ming dynasty novel *Chin P'ing Mei* ("The Golden Lotus") perhaps gives the best view of how money could be spent to corrupt the judicial process.[6]

Here is how the people recorded their love of a humane and just official (no. 16):

Sweet Pear Tree

> Don't chop that pear tree,
> Don't spoil that shade;
> Thaar's where ole Marse Shao used to sit,
> Lord, how I wish he was judgin' yet.

Chih: Education. Let us turn, then, from the first basis (*jen*) of personal virtue to the second basis, education or learning. China surely is unique among world cultures in the extent to which she has encouraged learning and has rewarded the educated. The mandarins really ran the country, and the rigorous system of examinations assured that they all were educated before they got any power. *The Book of Documents* says, "The king said, 'Study antiquity in order to enter on your offices. In deliberating on affairs, determine by help of such study, and your arts of government will be free from error.'"

The emperor himself often took pride in his ability to write verse—Ts'ao P'ei did although his brother Ts'ao Chih was better at it, Li Yü did and became one of the greatest poets although he lost the throne, the Ch'ien Lung emperor wrote several thousand verses and kept his throne, although some historians say that most of the thousands were written *for* him, and at least one poet was purged because he claimed to have written a poem which the Ch'ien Lung emperor also claimed.

The duke of Chou is one of China's archetypal "good rulers," although he only was regent for a time and never emperor. Confucius often refers to the duke of Chou, praising him for his benevolent and effective direction of the state, and it is the duke of Chou to whom Confucius refers in his famous remark, picked up by Yeats for the epigraph to *Responsibilities*: "How am I fallen from myself, for a long time now, I have not seen the Prince of Chang [= the duke of Chou] in my dreams." The duke of Chou is supposed to have written about 67 of the songs in *The Book of Songs* (*see* Chronology), i.e., one fifth of the total.

I: Equity. We may turn now to the third basis of *tê—i*, sometimes translated as "equity." Peter Boodberg recognizes that the concept *i* antedated in China the concept *jen,* or "humanitas." Working along etymological lines, Boodberg shows that the word *i* in Chinese almost certainly is cognate to the word *wo,* "we." Boodberg then defines *i* as "loyalty to the 'we-group'." Such is in keeping with early and enduring Chinese values, and we can find it illustrated by Confucius's conversation with Duke Sheh.[7]

Professor Boodberg holds that *jen* developed later as a concept, and he points to the recognized etymological relationship between *jen,* "humanitas," and *jen,* "people (in general), other people." Boodberg then defines *jen* (the virtue) as a sense of the community of all men, a sense of the generic affinity between all men. Confucius had the sense when he said, "Within the four seas, all men are brothers." The reader can easily see that to balance, or reconcile, the virtues *i* and *jen* is a great feat in human affairs.

In *The Book of Documents* the duke of Chou, instructing the king on training his officers and maintaining their merit, says of *i*: (1) "my young son, can you put up with inequity? If you do so, the consequences will be like a fire—a spark at first, which blazes up, and by-and-by cannot be extinguished." (2) "In the Ch'u history it is said: The Ch'u State does not go in for collecting wealth (treasuring procelain, jewels, and money), but counts fair-dealing its treasure." The *Great Learning* says "A state does not profit by profits. Equity is the treasure of states."

"Nine Meshes" is a poem in which the people sing the duke of Chou's praise (no. 159):

Nine Meshes

Nine meshes of the net enclose
two sorts of fishes, bream, these, rudd, those:
Behold our prince in his bright-broidered clothes.

Wild geese a-wing circle the isle;
The Duke's coming's so short a while;

Wild geese seek land as but a pause in flight;
Return, and not to be here but a night;

The Dragon-Robe in so brief a stay,
Who'd neither cause us grief, nor stay away.

The duke of Chou, according to tradition, was recalled to the West, and the folk in the East wrote this to express their regret at his leaving.

Li: Ritual and Manners. The fourth basis of *tê* is *li*. *Li* as a Confucian concept usually is defined as "rites, ritual, wisdom, manners, propriety." The graph for it is a picture of an emanation or spirit beside a ritual jar full of flowers—it could be a picture of the little shrine Chinese even today have in their houses, and where the *mater familias* night by night performs the ritual service for the ancestors. Of all Chinese rituals, this service to the ancestors is the most basic and important. The word *li* certainly is cognate to the *li*, meaning "veins in jade or principles," and this latter *li* is used by philosophers to mean "the principles binding things together." According to Confucian conviction, it is custom, manners, propriety, and rites as social activities which hold the social body together and cause it to continue to function and to prosper. The Confucian *li* runs from the emperor's plowing of the imperial furrow in the capital—a rite always performed when it was time for the farmers of China to begin their spring plowing—to the humblest ancestral service in the evening, in the smallest peasant's hut. The emperor was a cosmic figure, and it was part of his function to keep the three great realms of heaven, earth, and mankind operating in harmony. The rituals and rites which the emperor kept were the *means* whereby he tried to preserve and renew this harmony. The concept of *li*, however, is pervasive in Chinese culture and the concept itself is *very* broad and far-reaching.

The earliest extensive Chinese history book, *Mr. Left's History,* holds that *li* is the main operative force in history and sees men prosper or fail and nations rise or fall according to how much they have *li*. Burton Watson observes: "In many passages in [*Mr. Left's History*], this word *li* refers to the specific rules of conduct which govern religious and social ceremonies, the points of etiquette to be observed in public and private life. But in other passages . . . the word is expanded in meaning and scope until . . . [it] has become . . . . a comprehensive moral standard which embraces all phases of human behavior and even extends to the natural and supernatural worlds."[8] Thus, under Duke Chao's twenty-fifth year we read: "Ritual (*li*) is the constant principle of Heaven, the righteousness of Earth, and the proper action of mankind. . . . Ritual determines the relations of high and low; it is the warp and woof of Heaven and Earth and that by which the people live" (Watson, p. 45). Let us consider some poems in which *li* figures.

The poem "Green Robe" complains against Duke Chuang of Wei, for his lack of *li*. Duke Chuang had put out of his favor his number one wife's son and had replaced him with a lesser concubine's son. "Green Robe" complains against it[9] (no. 27):

Green Robe

Green robe, green robe, lined with yellow,
Who shall come to the end of sorrow?

Green silk coat and yellow skirt,
How forget all my heart-hurt?

Green the silk is, you who dyed it;
Antient measure, how divide it?

Nor fine nor coarse cloth keep the wind
from the melancholy mind;

Only antient wisdom is
solace to man's miseries.

The next poem, "The Tribulus Grows on the Wall," blames
Huan, son of the Duke Hsüan. Although the poem sounds like
a poem of general complaint against general bad standards in
the women's quarters, the tradition has it that Huan was sleeping
with one of his father's concubines, I Chiung. Naturally, if the
affair were known to various people at the court, even such a
poem of "general complaint" would be understood by everyone
as referring to the scandal of the son and the concubine (no. 46:
my translation):

The Tribulus Grows on the Wall

The Tribulus grows on the wall.
Pull not this vine away.
The things they do in the harem—
Give not the tale away.
The things they do in the harem—
There is no shame to the things.

The Tribulus grows on the wall.
Pull not the vine away.
The things they do in the harem—
Give not the truth away.
The things they do in the harem—
There is no end to the things.

The tribulus grows on the wall.
Pull not the vine away.
The things they do in the harem—
Give not the tale away.
The things they do in the harem—
There is no grace to the things.

Here is another poem (no. 52), where the poet criticizes a
man for his lack of *li*:

A Rat Too

A rat too has a skin (to tan)
A rat has a skin at least
But a man who is a mere beast
might as well die,
his death being end of no decency.

A rat also has teeth
but this fellow, for all his size, is beneath
the rat's level,
why delay his demise?

The rat also has feet
but a man without courtesy need not wait
to clutter hell's gate.

Why should a man of no moral worth
clutter the earth?
This fellow's beneath the rat's modus,
why delay his exodus?

A man without courtesy
might quite as well cease to be.

We find that the concept of *li* is always there in Chinese life. To bear sons is one of the Chinese wife's important functions, but it is not the only important one. We already have said that the mother, in a Chinese family, performs the service to the ancestors nightly. A Chinese, then, must find a wife worthy to perform these ancestral services—or rather, his parents must find such a worthy wife, and this may be an important reason why Chinese parents took, and take, such a dominant role in arranging a marriage. The poem "How Cut Haft" (no. 158) shows, in its last line, how much stress was laid on the bride's fitness to perform the rituals: [10]

How Cut Haft?

How cut haft for an axe?

Who hacks
holds a haft.
To take a wife
properly
one gets a notary.

To hack an axe-haft
an axe
hacks;
the pattern's near.

I have found her at last:
food stands
in the ritual dish.

The "notary" is the "go-between" or *mei-jen* who in China traditionally arranged marriage and negotiated terms between the two families.

The lines "To hack an axe-haft/ an axe/ hacks;/ the pattern's near" have become proverbial, and—like all good proverbs— they are used with application to many another subject than that to which they first were applied. The lines are quoted in the seventh of the thirteen Confucian classics, *The Book of Rites*, and in the later condensation known as the *Chung Yung*, or *Unwobbling Pivot*: "To hack an axe-haft/ an axe/ hacks;/ the pattern's near. One seizes one axe-handle in cutting the other. One can, at a glance, note a divergence from the model. Thus the man of breed uses men in governing men."[11]

If the emperor properly performs the rituals, heaven, earth, and man will stay in harmony, and disasters and calamities will not occur. Here is a poem (no. 251) on the blessings of the benevolent ruler:

Dip the Flood Water Up

Cleared by its flowing, dip the flood water up
and it will steam thy rice or other
grain; a deferent prince is
to his people both father and mother.

Rain-water cleared by its overflood
if thou ladle it out will wash thy altar jar;
To a fraternal prince will his folk
return, as to home from afar.

In a fraternal prince his folk have rest,
as from rain water
cleared by its flowing thou hast
a pure house, or thy garden is blest.

The lines "A deferent prince is/ to his people both father and mother," unless they were proverbial before and the poet picked them up, went thereafter into China's proverb-inventory. The idea that the ruler is, or should be, like "father and mother" to his people comes up again and again in Confucian doctrine. *The Great Learning*, quoting "High Hill" (no. 172), says: " 'What a joy are these princes/ at once father and mother of their people.' To love what the people love and hate what is bad for the

people [what they hate] is called being the people's father and
mother. ... To love what the people hate, to hate what they
love is called doing violence to man's inborn nature. Calamities
will come to him who does this [definite physical calamities],
the wild grass will grow over his dead body" (*ibid.*, pp. 69
and 81).

The Shang dynasty kings were hunters. They made some of
the most beautiful bronzes men have ever made. When the
Shang dynasty was overthrown, in the battle on Mu Plain in
spring, 1122 B.C., China was in for profound changes. The rulers
of the new dynasty, the Chou dynasty, hunted less and farmed
more. Under the Chou rule, an agricultural society came to
predominate. The brilliance of the Chou dynasty shone through
in its literature, of which the brightest example is *The Book
of Songs.*

The "patron deity" of the Chou rulers was Hou Chi, "Lord
Grain." The final section of *The Book of Songs* is called "Odes
of the Temple and Altar." Let us look at an ode from that
section: "Think to Thine Art" (no. 275, "The Temple Odes of
Chou"). It has special ritual significance in that it was probably
performed for services to the "Lord Grain":

Think to Thine Art

> Think to thine art, Lord Grain.
> By thy power to drink down
> cup for cup of heaven's own
> stablish thou us by damp and heat.
> Without thee is naught complete,
> barley and wheat from thee we cull,
> Over-sky gave thee the rule
> how to feed us. Lead us,
> not by this field bourne held in,
> that the fruitage ever run
> in seasons of the Hia's sun.

The "Hia" mentioned in this last line is the Chou Kingdom.

V   *Ruler and Ministers*

We can understand from the following speech the importance
which the rulers of old attached to ministers. The king says to
his prime minister: "Suppose me a weapon of steel;—I will use

you for a whetstone. Suppose me crossing a great stream,— I will
use you for a boat with its oars. Suppose me in a year of great
drought; I will use you as a copious rain" (*Documents,* IV, viii).
The matter of ministers can be considered as two separate problems: selection of them, relations with them.

The *Documents* contain these remarks on the selection of
ministers: (1) "The sovereign should share his government with
none but worthy ministers. The worthy minister should accept
his support only from the proper sovereign." (2) The duke of
Chou said to Prince Shih, "If you can but reverently cultivate
your virtue, and bring to light our men of eminence. . . ." The
latter point—"bring to light our men of eminence"—is especially
interesting, in light of the *modern* theory that revolution does
not get started among the oppressed masses, but rather gets
started among some capable and gifted group, the members of
which feel they aren't getting their due under the present
system.

Here is one poem about a ruler who evidently has neglected
to "share his government only with worthy men" (no. 18):

Fleecy Coats

In fleecy coats with five white tassels,
affable snakes, the great duke's vassals glide
from his hall
to tuck their court rations inside.

In lambskin coats with five wider tassels,
affable snakes, the duke's vassals all
glide out to dinner
on leaving the hall.

With quadruple tassels or seams to their coats,
lambskin and all, with that elegant look,
noble vassals, affable snakes
glide out to consume what they get from the duke.

It is a basic tenet of Confucianism that "There are five relations
of great importance under Heaven: ruler and minister, father
and sons, husband and wife, elder brother and younger brother,
and friend and friend." In the *Documents,* on the relation of
prince and minister, the king said to his prime minister: "Do
you teach me what should be my aims. Be to me as the yeast

and the malt in making sweet spirits; as the salt and the prunes in making agreeable soup. Give your help to cultivate me" (IV, VIII).

We can see from the poem "Castrato" how one Meng Tsy (a much earlier figure than the philosopher) continues to remonstrate with, and to try to educate, his government, even after his past effort had brought great calamity upon him (no. 200). And we can see how one man kept the Confucian precept: "Tzu-lu asked about serving one's prince. Confucius said, 'Don't cheat him. Withstand him to his face'" (*Analects*, XIV, 23). Here is the poem:

Castrato

Such elegant streaky lines in brocade
till the solid shell is made;
liars by littles ply their trade.

Stitch a-sky, dot, the South Sieve's made.
Who loves to aid
these smearers in the smearing trade?

Winging,
gad about,
tittling, tattling
to be found out.

The quickness of the hand deceives the eye
and repetition suaves mendacity,
unopposed, you'll be ousted bye and bye.

Proud men ride high to watch the workers sweat,
O'er-hanging heaven look down upon their pride
and pity those on whom the yoke is set.

Take therefore, I say, these smearers
and fellow travellers, chuck 'em
to wolves and tigers, and if the striped cats spew 'em forth,
offer 'em to the Furthest North.
If the old pole decline to spare 'em place,
kick 'em clean off into stellar space.

And here's my address, I am still
at Willow Hollow Road by Acre Hill,
Meng Tsy has lost his balls but makes this verse,
let the administration heed it, or hear worse.[12]

The title, and the penultimate line, allude to the ancient practice of locking up political prisoners and leaving them with the means to commit suicide. If the prisoner was still alive after a certain time, he was taken from his cell and castrated.[13]

The theme of slander against worthy men at court is one of the most important themes in Chinese literature and history. The *Li Sao* by "China's first poet," Ch'ü Yuan, deals with the theme at great length. Anyone who has read Lin Yutang's *The Gay Genius*, a biography of the Sung dynasty poet Su Tung-p'o, can see that slander was a theme of literature because it was a fact of life. Many careers were reversed or ruined because of slander. If the reader has seen the Japanese film *Seven Who Tread the Tiger's Tail*—which itself is based on a kabuki play— he may remember that the trouble all was caused by "slander at court." So did Japanese literature inherit from the Chinese this preoccupation. We find it as a theme in Chinese literature as early as *The Book of Songs*. "Blue Flies" presents it (no. 219):

Blue Flies

Flies, blue flies on a fence rail
should a prince swallow lies wholesale?

Flies, blue flies on a jujube tree,
slander brings states to misery.

Flies, blue flies on a hazel bough
even we two in slanderers' row
                    B'zz, b'zz, hear them now.

CHAPTER 3

War

THE Chinese populace, in its history, has often suffered terribly from war. The common Chinese might expect to be drafted, for warfare or for forced labor. Pearl Buck has described how it still was, early in this century:

> He saw one day, when he pulled his ricksha empty down a street looking for a customer, a man seized as he stood by a small band of armed soldiers, and when the man protested, the soldiers brandished knives in his face, and while Wang Lung watched in amazement, another was seized and another, and it came to Wang Lung that those who were seized were all common fellows who worked with their hands, and while he stared, yet another man was seized, and this one a man who lived in the hut nearest his own against the wall. Then Wang Lung perceived suddenly out of his astonishment that all these men seized were as ignorant as he as to why they were thus being taken, willy nilly, whether they would or not. And Wang Lung thrust his ricksha into a side alley and he dropped it and darted into the door of a hot water shop lest he be next and there he hid, crouched low behind the great cauldrons, until the soldiers passed.[1]

It was the proverb in China that you only use for soldiers "men like nails, you couldn't make anything else out of." But if the mandarins—like judges, police, legislators today—were not conscripted, most of them identified with and pitied the common man who was drafted, and they wrote many poems to protest it. Tu Fu (712-70) has written this poem that may be typical of their attitude (it is, of course, not a poem from *The Book of Songs*):

"Night in the Pavilion by the River"

Evening haze creeps up hill paths,
I lie in the pavilion overlooking
The river; light clouds envelop
Cliff sides, and the moon's reflection

Is twisted by the waters;
Cranes and storks rest after
Their flight; wild beasts howl
As they seek their prey; sleep
Does not come to me, for still
I worry about war, knowing I have
No way to set the world aright.[2]

But of the many, many Chinese antiwar poems, a great proportion—especially in *The Book of Songs* (of course)—was written
by the commoners. "Mao Mount" (no. 37) shows us how the
common soldier felt and what he thought about war.

Mao Mount

Mao Mount's vine-joints show their age,
Uncles and nobles, how many days?

Why delay here with no allies;
Why delay here in lack of supplies?

Fox furs worn thru, without transport,
Uncles and nobles, sorry sport!

We be the rump of Li with tattered tails,
a lost horde amid fears,
and your embroidered collars
cover your ears.

We can shift the focus here to the home front. We find another
folk poem written about other aspects of war and war's suffering (no. 66):

"He's to the War"

He's to the war
for the duration
Hens to wall-hole,
beasts to stall,
shall I not remember
him at night-fall?

He's to the war
for the duration,
fowl to their perches,
cattle to byre;

        is there food enough;
        drink enough
        by their camp fire?

The poem "Over the Hills" is especially effective because it keeps the battlefield and the home front tensely together in the poem. It also tells, or tries to tell, "the whole story," as it were.[3] The poet, as a young conscript, thinks of home as he marches out to the frontier (no. 110):

Over the Hills

On and on, over tree-covered hills
Look away and think of your father.
Your father will say, "Aiya!
"My own son has marched off to war
"And early and late, he will not rest.
"God, I hope he will keep his head
"And will come home and won't stay on."

On and on, over treeless hills.
Look away and think of your mother.
Your mother will say, "Aiya!
"My own baby has marched to war
"And early and late, he'll never sleep.
"God, I hope he will keep his head,
"Will come home, and won't get cut off."

On and on, over rocky spurs
Look away and think of your brothers.
Your brothers will say, "Aiya!
"Our kid brother has marched off to war
"And early and late, he'll hang in there.
"God, I hope he will keep his head
"And will come home, and won't get killed."

The student who wants to compare Chinese culture to American culture may set against this poem E. E. Cummings's "my sweet old etcetera."[4]

I   *Soldiers and Land Reclamation*

The following poem—one of the most famous of all Chinese poems—presents the soldiers' suffering. It also alludes to the age-old practice that the soldiers farmed the land they held.

They often reclaimed or claimed land for the agricultural Chinese society and populace, while they defended it against the barbarian hordes (no. 167):

Pick a Fern

Pick a fern, pick a fern, fern sprouts rise,
"Home," I'll say: home, the year's gone by,
no house, no roof, these huns on the hoof.
Work, work, work, that's how it runs,
We are here because of these huns.

Pick a fern, pick a fern, soft as they come,
I'll say "Home."
Hungry all of us, thirsty here,
no home news for nearly a year.

Pick a fern, pick a fern, if they scratch,
I'll say "Home," what's the catch?
I'll say "Go home," now October's come.
King wants us to give it all,
no rest, spring, summer, winter, fall,
Sorrow to us, sorrow to you.
We won't get out of here till we're through.

When it's cherry-time with you,
we'll see the captain's car go thru,
four big horses to pull that load.
That's what comes along our road,
What do you call three fights a month,
and won 'em all?

Four car-horses strong and tall
and the boss who can drive 'em all
as we slog along beside his car,
ivory bow-tips and shagreen case
to say nothing of what we face
sloggin' along in the Hien-yün war.

Willows were green when we set out,
it's blowin' an' snowin' as we go
down this road, muddy and slow,
hungry and thirsty and blue as doubt
(no one feels half of what we know).[5]

II *War and Famine*

Let us compare "Pick a Fern" and the other poems above to a later poem (not from *The Book of Songs*), still by one of the common folk in which war's sorrow is sung. It is "country music" —that is, a "Music Bureau piece"—from about the third century, maybe earlier. The last two lines are often quoted.

They Fought South of the City

We fought in the south
Died in the north
Field-slain, unburied, crows devour us.
For us, tell the crows:
"For you we stay.
"Shall rotten flesh get away?"

. . .

God, my God—
What good south;
North, what good?
Corn, wheat unreaped—the lord's food.
We would be true men if we could.

Envoi

Learn: you were good men.
Good men surely shall learn:
Dawn, go out to battle;
Dusk, you shall not return.[6]

When the soldiers say, "Corn, wheat unreaped—the lord's food/ We would be true men if we could"—when thus with bitter irony he "apologizes," he speaks of the labor or its fruits conventionally owed by the people to the government or to the aristocracy. He also juxtaposes, by suggestion, the twin scourges of the Chinese people through history: war and famine, and as the Chinese have often noted, they often come together. Lao-tzu says, "Where an army camps, thorns and brambles grow./ After a great war, come years of famine." The two calamities are put together in "Lily bud floating" (no. 233):[7]

Lily bud Floating

Lily bud floating, yellow as sorrow,
grief today, what of tomorrow?

Gone the bud, green the leaf,
better unborn that know my grief.

Scrawny ewes with swollen heads,
the fish traps catch but stars.

What man has food now
after these many wars?

III   *"Patriotism"*

Of all these poems of protest against war, "The Buzzards Fly"
probably is, to the Confucian Chinese, the strongest statement.
For it suggests that the war has struck at the very roots of
society: the children's obligation to serve the ancestors and to
support the parents (no. 121):

The Buzzards Fly

Flapping, flapping the buzzards fly
They settle on the bushy oaks.
Working for the King, there's no rest.
Now we cannot tend our grain;
How shall the parents be sustained?
Grief, grief. O blue Sky
When will these things, too, pass by?

Flapping, flapping the buzzards sail
They settle on the bushy thorn-trees.
Working for the King, there's no rest.
Now we cannot tend our grain;
How shall the parents be maintained?
Grief, grief. O blue Sky
When will these things, too, go by?

Flapping, flapping the buzzards line up.
They settle on the bushy mulberries.
Working for the King, there's no rest.
We cannot plant millet or rice
What shall the parents have to eat?
Grief, grief. O blue Sky,
When will these things be set right?[8]

To be sure, in Chinese literature there are some few poems
that have a less negative attitude toward war. Poem 262 cele-

brates Chou victories in a war of defense against the South
tribes (825 B.C.):

> Kiang and Han
> > crashing along,
> A river of men
> > flowing as strong,
> Never a stop,
> > never astray,
> When we went out a-hunting
> > the wild tribes of the Huai.
> Out with our cars
> falcon-flags clack,
> never a halt,
> no broken rank,
> when we marched to outflank
> > the wild tribes of the Huai.

> 2

> Turgid the waters of Kiang and Han,
> a glitter of men
> > flow rank upon rank.
> As threads on a loom
> > done as to plan,
> We sent dispatches up to the throne:
> "The four coigns are quiet,
> in four coigns no riot,
> Let the King's commons live quiet."
> There was, so, for a time no unsettlement
> and the King's mind was content.
> . . .

And Lu Yu (1122-1210), one of China's most prolific and
respected poets, has sung of military glory, or at least of the
political and territorial power which is (perhaps) its conse-
quence. But I can think of only one major poem in which the
poet seems to sing the soldier's glory straight out. It is the
eleventh of "The Nine Songs" from *The Elegies of Ch'u*:

Pro Patria Mori

> They shake their clamorous spears,
> > they have hide jackets and shields.
> They drive the chariots together,
> > they cross the short swords.

Their banners cover the sun,
            their enemies move like clouds.
Arrows—criss, cross—fall,
            the soldiers move on and on.
They overrun our patrols,
            they break across our lines.
Leftward, the horses fall
            rightward, the blades draw blood.
The chariot-wheels are blocked
            and hang on the coupled horses.
Draw out the sticks of jade,
            strike the strident drum.
Heaven times the fall;
            the dangerous gods are mad.
They are bitterly slain to the last
            and strewn on the open fields.
They joined and shall not rejoin,
            turned out and do not return.
The flats stretch on without end,
            the road leaps over the earth.
They wore, at the belt, long swords,
            and under each arm, thick bows.
Their bodies and heads are disjoined,
            their hearts shall never defer.
Yea, they were bold in extreme;
            again and again they armed.
To the end, they were haughty and hard;
            none could bring them down.
Their bodies indeed are gone;
            the gods will gather their souls,
Drive the unbodied ghosts,
            make heroes among the dead.[9]

This attitude is *not* typically Chinese. We find in "Cranes and Geese" a more typical Chinese attitude to such breast thumping (no. 181):

Cranes and Geese

Cranes and geese are flying,
And each wing tilts and lifts.
Your sons are on the march.
We fight and sweat in the wilds.
Weep for them, even these men
And cry for the children and wives.

Cranes and geese are flying
and flock in the heart of the marsh.
Your sons are at the sides,
The fifty-foot walls are raised.
Though we have sweated and fought,
Shall we live, in the end, in peace?

Cranes and geese, still flying,
Cry, grieving, knaw! knaw!
There are those, intelligent men,
That speak of us sweating and beat.
There are those, ignorant men,
That speak of our "glory" and "aims."[10]

We can find much the same attitude fifteen hundred years
later in Li Po. He wrote this poem in imitation of "They Fought
South of the City" (cited above):

"They Fought In the South"
Last year, we attacked
    at Mulberry Flats and its springs;
This year, we attack
    on the Onion River roads.
At the T'iao-chih sea,
    We wash our swords in the surf;
At Heaven's Hills,
    We pasture our horses to snow and grass.

Three thousand miles—
    hang on, march and attack.
Three armies—everyone
    cut up or grown old.
Barbarian gangs
    take slaughter and carnage
        as plowing and craft.
From of old, they have only sown
    white bones on their yellow sand-fields.

The House of Ch'in hammered up walls
    to hold off the hordes—and there
The House of Han still keeps
    flickering beacon-fires.
Flickering beacon-fires never cease:
March, attack—
    it's always the season for wars.

On the field:
         Attack! Grapple! Struggle! Die!
Knocked-down horses shriek, whine
         and cry to the sky.
Crows, kites peck human bowels;
carrying them, they fly
         and lay them on dead tree and branch.

Lieutenants, privates
         stain the grass and weeds.
Generals! Secretaries!
         what good does this do?
So we know:
         these so-called "arms"
                  are really murderer's tools.
Benevolent men
         seek for them
                  neither use nor excuse.[11]

The Chinese are loyal primarily to the family; they recognize religious duties to the ancestors. No doubt this has done much to determine the Chinese attitude toward war and war's folly.

CHAPTER 4

Separation

OF all the subjects on which Chinese poets have composed
their poems, two have been the most frequently used:
separation and war's misery. A Chinese poet may write of separation from any human being, naturally, with whom his own happiness, his own delight in life, is connected. The Western reader
will find that the Chinese poets write, much more frequently
than the Western poets, of separation from a friend.

Let us first take up poems in which the poet is separated from
spouse or lover. In poem 33, a lady laments that her husband,
being sent away on government business, is separated from her.
The "hundred gentlemen" is taken to be the powerful ministers
surrounding the emperor. We may assume, since the wife complains to them as she does in the last stanza, that her husband, in
fact, has been sent into temporary exile.

Pheasant-cock

Pheasant-cock flies on easy wing,
Absent lord, to my sorrowing.

As the bright pheasant flies
wind lowers and lifts the tone;
sorrow: my lord gone out,
I am alone.

Look up to the sun and moon
in my thought the long pain,
the road is so long, how
shall he come again.

Ye hundred gentlemen, conscienceless
in your acts, say true:
He neither hates nor covets,
what wrong shall he do?

43

Considering the frequency with which the imperial government conscripted armies and public-work forces (for such projects as canal building and flood control), we should not be surprised to find that conscriptees, or their wives, wrote "poems of separation" about their situation and its grief. For example, there is "Rapids float no fagot here" (no. 68). The translator assumes that the poem mentions "some sort of water-post," as in the Tristan and Isolde legends. Whether or not he assumes correctly, we may note that the streams grow shallower and shallower, as they would when the army moved westward from the settled plains to uncivilized areas and then to areas settled by the barbarian hordes.

Rapids float no fagot here

Rapids float no fagot here
nor can she guard Shen frontier.
   Heart, O heart, when shall I home?

Ripples float no thorn-pack thru
nor will she fight by us in Fu.
   Heart, O heart, when shall I home?

Freshets float no osier here
nor can she guard Hü frontier.
   Heart, O heart, when shall I home?[1]

"Plucking the vine-leaves" is another favorite and famous "poem of separation" from *The Book of Songs* (no. 72):

Plucking the Vine Leaves

Plucking the vine leaves, hear my song:
"A day without him is three months long."

Stripping the southernwoods, hear my song:
"A day without him is three autumns long."

Reaping the tall grass hear my song:
"A day without him 's three years long."

The reader will note for himself that the poetess expresses with increasing intensity the pain of her separation: ". . . months . . . autumns . . . years." The line "A day without him 's three years long" has become a cliché in Chinese literature and speech.

We should note that in "poems of separation," separation of spouse from spouse is not the only subject. In later Chinese poetry, poems of separation most often deal with separation of friend from friend.

In the song "Swallows, Swallows" (no. 28) a lady watches her best friend leave for a new husband's home. As do many poems of separation, "Swallows, Swallows" shows the age-old Chinese custom of *sung* (rhymes with Jung). To *sung* someone is to accompany him part way on his trip. Chinese roadways traditionally are dotted, outside the cities, with little way stations and inns, so that *sung* parties may stop and have a farewell cup of wine before the traveler parts finally from his friends. It is still a Chinese custom to *sung* party guests, to accompany them to the curb side where their car is.[2] Here are the first three stanzas:

Swallows, Swallows

Swallows on swallows fly, fly.
Zig, zag go their wings.
She shall go to her new home.
I go along into the waste
And gaze till she fades from sight
And tears fall like the rain.

Swallows on swallows fly, fly.
They straighten their necks, they stretch their necks.
She shall go to her new home.
Into the distance, I follow her
And gaze till she fades from sight
And stop and stand and weep for it.

Swallows on swallows fly, fly.
Rising, falling, are their voices.
She shall go to her new home.
I go along far to the South
And gaze till she fades from sight
And this thing works on my heart.

Especially during the T'ang dynasty (618-906), the poets wrote poems of separation. The most popular T'ang anthology is modeled on *The Book of Songs* at least to the extent of being called "*The* Three Hundred T'ang Poems" (for Confucius calls *The Book of Songs* "*The* Three Hundred Poems"). Here are a couple of poems of separation from *The Three Hundred T'ang Poems*. They deal with the moment just before or after the *sung* was over. The usual title for such poems is "I *sung* so-and-so at such-and-such a place," and the T'ang poets turned out hundreds of them. Whether or not the Western reader appreciates the conceit in "the crybaby candle" will depend on his individual poetic taste and education. To read here this T'ang poem, after having read by now many *Book of Songs* poems, may help the reader to see the development, or deliquescence, of Chinese poetry from Confucius's time to that of the T'ang.

Going-away Gift
(Tu Mu, 803-52)

When we're most moved,
We often seem
Most unmoved.

We sit with wine
and talk all night
(but no one smiles).

Maybe the candle
knew we said
goodbye, maybe

the bitter wax
was tears. Look—
a white sky.[3]

Maybe the poet himself was embarrassed when he had conceived the figure, and sought a little to distract us with his sudden white sky.

Li Po (699-762) wrote one of the most famous of all poems of separation. It also can be found in *The Three Hundred T'ang Poems*. The "Meng" whom Li Po mentions is another T'ang poet.

I 'Sung' Meng Hao-jan at Gold Crane Tower

You travelled west
from Gold Crane Inn

Down Yang Chou
where flowers are like mist.

> And I see
> a sail's far shadow fly
> against green air,
>
> Then only the stretching
> river, and the empty sky.[4]

But perhaps in all Chinese poetry, the most beloved poem of separation was written by Emperor Li Yü (936-78) of the Southern T'ang dynasty (937-75). It is written, ironically I suppose, to fit a song called "Meeting's Pleasure." Millions of Chinese know it by heart:

To the Tune of "Meeting's Pleasure"

> Without words, alone
> I climb the West tower.
> The moon is like a hook.
> The *wu-t'ung* trees
> are lonely.
> The close garden locks in
> The clear autumn.
>
> Scissored and unsevered,
> Settled yet dishevelled,
> Is parting's sorrow;
> 'Separate,' a sort of odd taste
> On the heart's edge.[5]

The Book of Songs also has in it many poems of separation in which the poet (or poetess) misses his family and kin. The poetess of "Spring Water" has been married and, like all Chinese women when they marry, has become part of the husband's family. Chinese women sometimes thus were separated virtually for good from the kith and kin with whom they had been raised, and we may imagine that the period of adjustment was prolonged and difficult. We can get of this separation and adjustment, a clearest picture from the poem "Spring Water" (no. 39). The "farewell cup" is the *sung* cup which we mentioned above.

Spring Water

> Ware spring water that flows to the K'i,
> flowing thought is jeopardy.
> Every day my thought's in Wei,
> where pretty cousins would talk to me
> we would devise right pleasantly.

To Tsy for the night, and farewell cup at Ni;
When a girl marries she goes out
far from her parents and close male kin;
there's a feast and she
asks her aunts and sisters all in.

Now I would night by Kan and Yen.
"Grease the axle and fit the lynch-pin"
anything to get quickly to Wei
without roadside calamity.

"By Fei-Ts'üan's winding stream"
of Sü and Ts'ao is all my dream,
and all I can get is a p.m. drive
to keep my inner life alive.

It is a stock situation of Chinese literature that the new
bride finds, of all things, adjusting to her mother-in-law most
difficult. One historian put it that the bride became a virtual
servant to her husband's mother. If this is an overstatement,
nevertheless it is true that the critical relation in determining a
woman's success as wife more likely would be with her parents-
in-law than with her spouse. Maybe the poetess of "Spring Water"
suffers too in this classic dilemma.

China has regional differences just as the United States does;
regional differences may in fact be more pronounced in China
than in the American republic. Of course, the multitudinous
dialects of China—they are cognate languages like English and
Dutch rather than dialects like Southern American English and
Boston English—China's dialects give us the most dramatic
example of regional difference. A Chinese saying has it, "Travel
forty miles, you won't understand two words," but the language
situation really is not that bad. Differences of temperament and
value also are supposed to distinguish region from region. And
where the Northern Chinese tend to call themselves "men of
Han," after one of China's most famous dynasties, Southern
Chinese may say they are "men of T'ang," after the other famous
dynasty four hundred years later.

It came to be a practice in the Chinese civil service to shift
magistrates and governors around every three years and never
to let them hold office in their home area so that they would
be less tempted and less temptable. Whether or not this was
regular government practice in the seventh century B.C., the author

of "Yaller Bird" (no. 187) found himself an unpopular government official in an alien area. Ezra Pound translated the poem in Southern dialect because of an ancient tradition about the origin of the song and its author. The poet in lines one and two probably is quoting the local citizenry's unfriendly address to him, and "yaller bird" may be a racial or regional epithet. The true Chinese complexion is suffused almond, and the Chinese themselves regard a "yellow face" as unbeautiful. Northern Chinese tend to be paler than Southerners.

Yaller Bird

"Yaller bird, let my corn alone,
Yaller bird, let my crawps alone,"
These folks here won't let me eat,
I wanna go back whaar I can meet
the folks I used to know at home,
      I got a home an' I wanna' git goin'.

"Yalla' bird, let my trees alone,
Let them berries stay whaar they'z growin'.'"
These folks here ain't got no sense,
can't tell 'em nawthin' without offence,
Lemme, lemme, le'mme go home.
      I got a home an' I wanna' git goin'.

"Yaller bird, you stay outa dem oaks,
Yalla' bird, let them crawps alone."
I just can't live with these here folks,
    I gotta home and I want to git goin'
    To whaar my dad's folks still is a-growin'.[6]

We should also consider, as part of "Yaller Bird's" content, the inveterate and even bitter nostalgia which Chinese have for their home village or region. So natural to Chinese is this sense of personal roots, that the standard biographical form—even in a dictionary where the entry will be limited and may deal with someone of a millennium ago—begins by specifying the area of China to which the person is attached. I say "attached" because it may not be the place where he himself was born: his *ancestors'* home is his home village. The poem below by Wang Yun (1228-1306) is a fine poem on this subject. The reader will notice for himself the dramatic peripeteia, or reversal of direction, between lines six and seven.

To the Tune: "The Little Peach is Red"

Lotus-pickers' voices come through the autumn mist.
The waves are as still as cross-run silk.
Put your hand into wind and light, neither flows away—
Both flow on and on.
On the painted boat, you suddenly smile
              for the Spring wind on your face.
The river and hills are beautiful indeed,
But this is not my land—
When will the year come I may go home?

CHAPTER 5

"Love . . ."

—Sing we a song for love and idleness,
Naught else is worth the having.

IT may be that Dante *was* putting down Aristotle when he
called him "maestro di color che sanno"—"master of those who
know." The angels do not "know," they love. Confucius makes
a perhaps even more interesting remark on love, more interesting
perhaps, in that it suggests a three-part hierarchy: "Those who
know," says Confucius, "are inferior to those that love; and those
that love, are inferior to those that delight in." The word here
translated as "love" is graphed with a woman beside a child.
The word here translated as "delight in" is written with a graph
which is used to write the word for music: the graph depicts
musical paraphernalia, perhaps bells and a drum, on some kind
of stand. We do not know that the ancient words for "delight in"
and "music" were cognate, but we can speculate that Confucius
meant "it is a finer thing to respond to another person spon-
taneously, as to music, even than to fulfill your instinctive and
traditional obligations to him."

We use our English word "love" to cover a variety of emotions,
urges, and experiences. The Chinese use different words to keep
some of these separate. "To love" someone as "to 'make love' to
them," the Chinese can write with a graph which contains the
"enter" element and the "flesh" element. Although the graph and
word are not used in polite Chinese, the idea is very clear, and
the graph itself is even vivid. If the Chinese meant "love" as "to
esteem, to regard as meritorious, commendable, or good," he
could use the graph mentioned before—a woman beside a child.
The most common word for "to love" in modern Chinese is
graphed with two hands, one giving, one receiving an object
which on inspection, reveals itself to be a heart.

I *"Clouds and Rain"*

Among the many euphemisms with which the Chinese, like
fastidious peoples the world over, cover physical love, the

51

euphemism "clouds and rain" is probably the most often heard.
They call it "clouds and rain" because of an old legend: "Hsiang,
King of Ch'u, dreamed a girl visited him and offered him 'the
service of pillow and mat.' Before she left, the girl said, 'At dawn,
I am the Morning Cloud; at dusk, I am the Driving Rain.' "[1] The
Chinese ever since have spoken of "Clouds and Rain," or "the
game of Clouds and Rain."

For consideration in this section, I have selected those songs
which deal with "clouds and rain": "romantic" or sensual love.
Some of them—especially in the "Songs of Cheng" which Confucius wanted to "banish"—frankly deal with liaisons or extrasocial
attachments. Such songs present, more or less obviously, those
passions, those irrationalities which the Greeks called Aphrodite
and the Romans Venus. You will remember that Homer has
Helen repudiate Aphrodite, as maker of her troubles, when
Aphrodite would take her to Paris's bed; and Aphrodite comes
back, "Don't start up with me, foolish, or I will come greatly
to hate you, as I now love you greatly."[2] It is only recently that
Western man has returned to this awe, or this respect, for
physical love and its tyrannies.

The unknown poets who made "the songs," give us various
pictures of love, its delights and reverses. Among the most
beautiful poems that say the simple and eternal thing, "My
lady is loveliest of all," I would put the following (no. 93):

"The Eastern Gate"

At the Eastern Gate of the City
Are girls like the clouds of Spring.
But I disdain their charms
For in her white blouse and under her thick veil
My friend is far more beautiful.

At the tower and covering wall
Are girls like the flowers of Spring
But I disdain their charms
For in her white blouse and under her yellow skirt
My friend is sweeter still.[3]

We may divide "love's reverses" into various categories. Love
unrequited is one. Love opposed by one's family is another. Love
thwarted by an arranged marriage is still another category in
love's reverses. Of poems that describe love's reverses, many

more Chinese poems than Western poems fall into the latter two categories: love opposed by family, love thwarted by an arranged marriage. I am speaking of statistics now, and of short poems. Here is one of the songs which describes love unrequited, or disrequited (poem no. 86):

"The Con Artist"

The con artist won't talk when we meet.
Terrible!
        I can't even eat.
The con artist won't come to dinner.
And I'm getting
        thinner and thinner.[4]

I have tried, in this poem, and in later poems shall try, to use language closer to what we speak: for the songs, or at least the "Airs of the States," were made up by ordinary people not by the mandarins.

We can see in the poem below a clear case of "love opposed by family" (no. 76):

"Chung, You Stud"

Chung, you stud—Chung, be a doll.
Don't leap my wall
      don't break my pear.
I don't dare, lover—
      father and mother—

    Chung:
Will I ever hold you in my arms?

    Chung's Girl:
Father and mother
    —Listen to me—
What they'd say
    you don't want to hear.

Chung, you stud—you got no sense.
Don't leap my fence
      don't break our stair.
I don't dare, lover—
      my big brother . . .
Will I ever hold you in my arms?

... My big brother
          —Listen to me—
What he'd say

          Chung:
          I don't want to hear.

          Chung's Girl:
Chung, you stud—you got no cools.
Don't leap the rails
          don't break the bush.
I don't dare, lover—
          People will talk—

          Chung and Chung's Girl:
Hold me forever in your arms.

          Chung's Girl:
People will talk
          —Listen to me—
What they'll say

          Chung and Chung's Girl:
          we don't want to hear.[5]

Although the general "plot" of this poem is clear, the reader who wants consciously to follow it through, might skip ahead to glance at Chapter 11 on the "Composite Image." A reader having some sophisticated knowledge of cinematographic technique may not need or want to have the device explained.

From "Chung, You Stud," we cannot tell why the family opposes the lovers in their relationship. In Chinese society, such opposition may occur because the family has betrothed the girl to a son in some other family. Such arrangement of a marriage might take place very early in the child's life, even while the future bride and groom still were infants.[6] When children thus were wed, for family advantage or prejudice rather than for individual affinity and "love," much heartache naturally could ensue, and the tragedies which followed from arranged marriages became in Chinese literature a favorite theme. A long early ballad, irrelevantly entitled "Southeast the Peacock Flies," condemns the practice of arranged marriage and concludes with the lines, "This tale is a warning for the men of time to come;/

May they learn its moral and hold it safe in their hearts." It was almost two thousand years before men of times to come began to heed.

We might put, into this same category, love with which circumstances interfere, if the interfering circumstance is wedlock to another person. But such a theme abounds in literature East and West—many troubadours made it the main subject of their success—and we cannot blame on arrangement the fact that some marriages do not remain forever blissful. Here is a song that deals, apparently, with this situation (no. 99):

Sun's in the East

Sun's in the East,
her loveliness
Comes here
To undress.

Twixt door and screen
at moon rise
I hear
Her departing sighs.

The lady comes to her lover in early morning, and she leaves him in the evening. We must assume from this that other obligations, other necessities take her away for the nights. Chinese poets and Chinese novelists often have written of this situation.

We may find in later Chinese poetry that the poet explicitly adverts to erotic experience:

A 'Tzu Yeh' Song
(fourth century A.D.)

Autumn moon's
　　　　at the open shutter.
The light's put out,
　　　　sheer robes gone wide.
Within silk curtains,
　　　　someone smiles;
The lifted orchids come untied.[7]

But in *The Book of Songs,* and of all Chinese poems that deal with physical love, the majority—even in the "Peruser of Literature" emperor's all-erotic *Jade Terrace Anthology*—present the peripheries, the consequences rather than the thing itself. Whether the poet is dealing with erotic emotion, or some other emotion, we have come to value highly just this sort of restraint in Chinese poetry. Indeed, this restraint has led some people to think that the Chinese wrote no erotic poetry. They should read *The Elegies of Ch'u* or the "Tzu Yeh songs"—or even, with care, *The Book of Songs.*

II *Epithalamia and Other "Marriage Poems"*

No look at love poetry would be satisfactory if we omitted epithalamia and marriage poems. Here are a few poems written about what the Chinese call "life's *great* event": marriage. Scholars suppose that this first poem was written for the marriage of the Elegant King and T'ai-Szu in the twelfth century B.C. (no. 1):

"Kuan!" Cries the Hawk

"Kuan! Kuan!" The fish-hawk
Keeps to the river-strait.
Nilling-willing noble daughter,
Royal son's perfect mate.

Ragged, jagged hsing plants
Leftward, rightward drifting:
Nilling-willing noble daughter—
Waking-sleeping sought her
Sought her yet not got her
And waking-sleeping thought of her.
                    Iu-tsai! Iu-tsai!
Turning, churning, still distraughter

Ragged, jagged hsing plants
Leftward, rightward lifting:
Nilling-willing noble daughter,
Lute and zither brought her!

Ragged, jagged hsing plants
Leftward, rightward sifting:
Nilling-willing noble daughter,
Bells and drums, applaud her![8]

The poet in "Peach-tree Fair" (no. 6) implies a favorite comparison of Chinese poets: peach tree and bride.

Peach-tree Fair

O peach-tree thou art fair
to shine with flaming flower
that goest to wed
and order thy house and bower.

O peach-tree thou art fair
to promise solid fruit
that goest to wed
and order thy bower and house

O peach-tree thou art fair
as leaf on leaf in bough
that goest to wed
and order thy people and house.[9]

We read in the next poem (according to one interpretation, at least) how a lady watches her husband-to-be arrive. Her excitement mounts as he draws nearer and nearer, and she sees his cortege is grander and his equipage richer than she had dared at first to believe (no. 53):

The Ox-tail Flag

Flapping, flapping are the ox-tail flags.
They are in the suburbs of Sun.
With white silk they have braided them.
Fine horses—he has four of them
And he himself's a goodlooking man
What shall I give as a present to him?

Flapping, flapping are the falcon flags
They are past the outer wall.
With white silk they have corded them.
Fine horses—he has five of them.
And he himself's a goodlooking man
What shall I offer as a gift to him?

Flapping, flapping are the feather flags
They are past the inner wall.
With white silk they have tied things on.
Fine horses—he has six of them!
And he himself's a goodlooking man
What shall I have to say to him?[10]

III *"Seraglio Poetry"*

Because the institution of concubinage played so important a
role in Chinese life, and even in Chinese history, we might not
be surprised to find poems in which the concubines, their lives
and lots, are presented. We do in fact find many famous poems
and paintings which depict the harem-lady's life. In later periods
(beginning around the fifth century A.D.), Chinese poets wrote
so many poems on the harem lady's lot and life, that the "seraglio
poem" was recognized as a distinct genre. During the early sixth
century, a school of poets flourished which was dubbed the Seraglio school because of its fondness for this subject matter. A
modern Chinese critic has this to say about the Seraglio school
and its work: "they have as content the emotional description
of women's faces, women's dress, women's attitudes, and women's
sensibilities. Why, they'll look you in the face and write of
what women do in bed after drinking wine—even of physical
love!"[11]

Seraglio poetry occurs less frequently in earlier poetry, but
song no. 21 probably is the earliest example of the Seraglio poem.
The song is called "The Little Stars"—with emphasis I believe on
the epithet rather than on the noun. The Chinese have always
called the emperor's lesser wives and concubines "the little stars."

For the Occidental reader, concubinage as an institution will
seem alien and exotic, so let me interject before "The Little
Stars" a brief description of the institution and how it worked:

It will be recalled that the Chinese emperor was a cosmic figure,
the analogue here below of the pole star on high. All hierarchies,
all officialdom, all works and days, revolved around his solitary
eminence. It was therefore entirely natural that from time immemorial
the large number of women attending upon him should have been
regulated according to the principles of the numinous cosmism which
pervaded Chinese court life. Ancient texts give us remarkable insight
into the ranks of his consorts and concubines. Though their titles
differed considerably during the two millennia which followed the
first unification of the empire, the general order comprised one
empress, three consorts, nine spouses (etymologically protegées or
client ladies) twenty-seven beauties (concubines), and eighty-one
attendant nymphs (assistant concubines). The *Chou Li* (*Record of the
Rites of the Chou Dynasty*) even gives us what might be called a
pernoctation rota.

"The lower-ranking (women)" it says, "come first, the higher-ranking come last. The assistant concubines, eighty-one in number, share the imperial couch nine nights in groups of nine. The concubines, twenty-seven in number, are allotted three nights in groups of nine. The nine spouses and the three consorts are allotted one night to each group, and the empress also alone one night. On the fifteenth day of every month the sequence is complete, after which it repeats in the reverse order."

Thus it is clear that the women of highest rank approached the emperor at times nearest to the full moon, when the Yin influence would be at its height, and matching the powerful Yang force of the Son of Heaven, would give the highest virtues to children so conceived. . . . In the +9th century Pai Hsing-Chien complained that all these rules had fallen into disorder, saying:

"Nine ordinary companions every night, and the empress for two nights at the time of the full moon—that was the ancient rule, and the Duennas-Secretarial kept a careful record of everything with their vermilion brushes. . . . But alas, nowadays all the three thousand (palace women) compete in confusion. . . ."

What was at stake was the imperial succession. Chinese ruling houses did not always follow the primogeniture principle, and the eldest son of the empress was not necessarily the heir apparent. Towards the end of a long reign an emperor would have quite a number of princes from which to choose, and in view of the importance of State astrology in China from very ancient times it may be taken as certain that one of the factors in this choice was the nature of the asterisms which had been culminating at the time of the candidate's conception. Hence the importance of the records which had been kept by the Duennas-Secretarial.[12]

Here is "The Little Stars" itself:

The Little Stars

Trembling indeed
　　　　　are the little stars.
Now three, now five
　　　　　are in the east.
Hurry up, hurry up!
　　　　　Tonight they go,
Some early, some late,
　　　　　to see the duke.
Their lot
　　　　　is not the same.

Trembling indeed
　　　　　are the little stars.

There's Orion.
There's the Pleiades.
Hurry up, hurry up!
Tonight they go,
Catch their covers
and clutch their sheets.
Their lot
does not
match hers.[13]

CHAPTER 6

". . . And Idleness"

—Small boat floats like a lanthorn,
The flowing water clots as with cold.
And at San Yin
they are a people of leisure.[1]

I The Occasional Poem

THERE is in the Occident considerable prejudice against the "occasional poem"—against the poem that deals with the specifics, or even the minutiae, of life, even of everyday life. But critics more than poets may disdain the occasion, may prefer the generalized "idea" as subject matter for poems. Goethe ran into this preference and this disdain, and he spoke subjectively to it: "Alle meine Gedichte sind Gelegenheitsgedichte, sie sind durch die Wirklichkeit angeregt und haben darin Grund und Boden. Von Gedichten aus der Luft gegriffen halte ich nichts" (*Gespräche mit Eckermann*, September 18, 1823).

In the United States and Europe, some pretty good modern poetry has been written using occasion. Yeats seems not to have liked it: "It has," he writes, "sometimes seemed of late years, though not in the poems I have selected for this book, as if the poet could at any moment write a poem by recording the fortuitous scene or thought, perhaps it might be enough to put into some fashionable rhythm—'I am sitting in a chair, there are three dead flies on a corner of the ceiling.' "[2] We Americans, or at least my generation that has loved and learned from William Carlos Williams, may be better prepared to appreciate the occasional poem, or *Gelegenheitsgedichte*. Europeans and Australians seem still not to have responded to Williams, and I cannot tell whether they dislike his (what Yeats would call) "mirror poems," or if he just is too American for them. Take this:

Between Walls

the back wings
of the

61

> hospital where
> nothing
>
> will grow lie
> cinders
>
> in which shine
> the broken
>
> pieces of a green
> bottle[3]

We stand in the poet's shoes and see for a moment what the poet saw—share with another person for an instant some moment, if "trivial" still memorable, memorable and moving for some obscure motive of the soul. And I think that this is a fine thing. It might take Taoism to give us a philosophical grounding for such poetry, its importance (or even its poeticality).

Here from *The Book of Songs* (no. 63) is a poem about goofing off, of one sort or another:

Prowls Fox

> K'i dam, prowls fox,
> a heart 's to hurt
> and someone 's there has got no skirt.
>
> By the Ki's deep on the prowl;
> got no belt on, bless my soul.
>
> Tangle-fox by K'i bank tall:
> who says: got no clothes at all?

The Chinese emperor, by the Chinese regarded as a cosmic figure, began his day at sunrise. Now this meant that ministers, attendants, bureaucrats, and civil servants themselves had to get up pretty early to be there. The poem below (no. 100) presents one such official, who found his lady's bed so sweet he had trouble making it on time:

In the East, It Is Still Not Light

> In the East, it is still not light.
> He twists and turns his kilt and coat
> Twisting them, turning them,
> To the court they summon him.

In the East, there is still no sun.
He twists and turns his coat and kilt,
Turning them, twisting them,
To the court they order him.

He breaks the willows and the fenced-in flowers,
Now runs forth, now runs back,
Doesn't make it morning or night,
Comes too early and goes too late![4]

This subject has endured in Chinese poetry, in part no doubt because bureaucrats in the T'ang still left early for court, and their ladies lay in bed and resented it. Here is a poem from *The Three Hundred T'ang Poems*:

Good Reason

The wind screen,
delicate as lace,
pictures clouds:
she, also beautiful,

has reason
to fear short nights;
spring, come
to Phoenix streets

For without reason
she's married a man
of Gold Tortoise Rank,
who counts it better

to start
early to work
than to enjoy
perfumed sheets.[5]

The poet of the next poem (no. 140) idly watches the sun rise:

Neath East Gate Willows

Neath East Gate willows
'tis good to lie.
She said:
        "This evening."
        Dawn 's in the sky.

> Neath thick willow boughs
> 'twas for last night.
> Thick the close shade there.
> The dawn is axe-bright.

Idly, dejectedly, I see him sitting on the ground, his hands stuck out behind him. If there is some sort of drama in the poems above, yet many occasional poems—many fine occasional poems—present a nondramatic occasion, as does Williams's "Between Walls."

A watchman, who waited most of the night for some "Mr. Big" to arrive, wrote about his wait in "The Courtyard Torches" (no. 182):

The Courtyard Torches

> What of the night?
> It is not yet midnight
> The courtyard torches blaze
> His Excellency is coming.
> The bit-bells sound ts'iang! ts'iang!
>
> What of the night?
> The night is not yet done
> The courtyard torches fade.
> His Excellency is coming.
> The bit-bells sound ching! ching!
>
> What of the night?
> The night is almost gone.
> The courtyard torches smoke.
> His Excellency is coming
> There you can see the flags.[6]

Chinese poets have never disdained the occasional poem. They have, in fact, written millions of them. Two principles may be invoked to explain an occasional poem's power. One principle is poetical: "Poetry presents the thing in order to convey the feeling. It should be precise about the thing and reticent about the feeling."[7] Ford Madox Ford has written of the Chinese poets' skill "in the most difficult of all the world-poetic sides of technique, . . . [which] consists in getting exquisite poetic meaning out of the mere transcription of natural objects, without any comments or ejaculations whatsoever."[8] The other principle,

relevant to occasional poems and their power, is psychological.
The Italians understood it who say *dolce far niente*. Wallace
Stevens understands it when he writes, "The greatest poverty
is not to live in a physical world." Gregory Corso had it when
he wrote his lines "To stand on the street-corner waiting for no
one, that's power." Mankind delights in sitting around doing
nothing, and since goofing off is one of man's most intense and
cherished pleasures, why shouldn't it appear in his poetry?

Lao-tzu says, "The Tao speaks words that are thin and flavorless, unlikely to make the passing stranger pause." Chuang-tzu
says (Americans always think he's got it backward), "Friendship
with inferior men is sweet like wine; friendship with superior
men is flavorless like water." If much poetry everywhere is sweet
like wine, many of these Chinese occasional poems are flavorless
like water. They anticipate the haiku.

II   *Party Songs*

There are also poems written for parties. The following poem
no doubt was sung as a "welcomer," when the guests, or guest-
of-honor, arrived (no. 161):

Deer Sing

"Salt
lick!" deer on waste sing:
grass for the tasting, guests to feasting;
strike lute and blow
pipes to show how
feasts were in Chou,
            drum up that basket-lid now.

"Salt
lick!" deer on waste sing:
sharp grass for tasting, guests to feasting.
In clear sincerity,
here is no snobbery.
This to show how
good wine should flow
            in banquet mid true
            gentlemen.

"Salt
lick!" deer on waste sing,

k'in plants for tasting, guests to feasting;
beat drum and strumm
lute and guitar,
lute and guitar to get
deep joy where wine is set
mid merry din
let the guest in, in, in, let the guest in.

If "Deer Sing" was sung by the host and his party when the guests arrived, the next poem must have been sung by the guests for the host. It appears to have been sung later on in the party than "Deer Sing" (no. 170):

Fish To Net

Fine fish to net,
ray, skate;
Milord's wine is
heavy and wet.

Fish to trap,
bream, tench,
Milord has wine
to drink and quench.

Fine fish to trap
carp and mud-fish
Milor' has' wine
in quantities'h.

Food in plenty
say good food
Plenty of food
all of it good,

This the song each guest agrees on:
Milor's good food all fits the season.

Believe me, the guests sound as "out of it" in the Chinese as they do in this fine English version. Where the poems of *The Book of Songs* almost always are written entirely in four-syllable lines, the poet here has mixed-in lines of four, two, and three syllables. The stanza beginning "Food in plenty" is the same drunkish talking-around it in Chinese, too. "Fish to Net" is one

of the best drinking songs I know in any language. It can be
set against the Elizabethans' drinking songs:

> The drinkers of beer
> Did ne'er yet appear
> In matters of any weight:
> 'Tis wine that inspires,
> And quenches love's fires,
> Teaches fools how to rule a state;
> Maids ne'er did approve it
> Because they that love it,
> Despise and laugh at their hate!

III Carpe Diem

Of themes which all poets in all places have loved to sing,
none perhaps has been more served than the *carpe diem* theme:
catch the day, enjoy today what life offers, for no one can know
how many tomorrows there'll be for him. Omar Khayyám made
this "slender" content the basis of an enduring mastery, which
Edward FitzGerald turned into one of the most popular books
in the English language:

> Ah, but my Computations, People say,
> Reduced the year to better reckoning?—Nay,
>   'Twas only striking from the Calendar
> Unborn To-morrow, and dead Yesterday.

I suppose that the most common *carpe diem* poem is the
"come-on" poem—the lover beseeches his lady to give him "that
last proof of tenderness" and threatens her with the coming of
age. Edmund Waller wrote his very beautiful English poem on it:

> Go, Lovely Rose

> Go, lovely Rose!
> Tell her that wastes her time and me
> That now she knows,
> When I resemble her to thee,
> How sweet and fair she seems to be.

> Tell her that's young,
> And shuns to have her graces spied,
> That hadst thou sprung
> In deserts, where no men abide,
> Thou must have uncommended died.

Small is the worth
Of beauty from the light retired;
Bid her come forth,
Suffer herself to be desired,
And not blush to be admired,

Then die! that she
The common fate of all things rare
May read in thee;
How small a part of time they share
That are so wondrous sweet and fair!

Against this English poem on the theme, we may set "Plum
Time Now" (no. 20) from *The Book of Songs*. Although "Plum
Time Now" is, or pretends to be, written from the lady's point
of view, its implications are the same as those in "Go, Lovely
Rose":

"Plum Time Now"

"Oh soldier, or captain,
Seven plums on the high bough,
plum time now,
seven left here, 'Ripe,' I cry.

Plums, three plums,
On the bough, 'Plum time!' I cry.

'No plums now,' I cry, I die.
On this bough
Be no plums now."

Not all *carpe diem* poems are invitations to bed, direct or
implied. Some of them deal with other pleasures, other delights
which man, in his fragility, is advised to catch. "Thorn-elm
on Mountain" is an example of poems with this other focus
(no. 115):

Thorn-elm on Mountain

Thorn-elm on mountain, white elm on slope,
the clothes you never wear,
carriages idle there
be another's fact or hope
    when you are dead, who now but mope.

Kao tree on crest, shrub in low-land,
dust in your courtly dancing place,
bells on rack and drums unlaced
shall be others' jollity
    when you've proved your mortality.

Terebinth stands high on the crest, chestnut in vale,
wine thou hast and lutes in array,
undrunk, unstruck today.
Who makest not carouse:
    another shall have thy house.

"Chariots, Rank on Rank" (no. 126) is another poem in which we find the *carpe diem* theme:

Chariots, Rank on Rank

Chariots, rank on rank
with white-fronted horses;
You'd see Milord?
    Eunuchs are bosses.

Terebinth on the hill, chestnuts in valley;
Once you're inside, there are lutes in each alley.
    Delight, delight
    and the long night
            coming.

Mulberries on the crest,
willows in marsh-land valley,
    drum-beat and shamisan,
            dally, dally,
    Death's up the alley.

Now that we have taken stock of the universal *carpe diem* theme, how the Chinese poets present it in *The Book of Songs*, we should find it very revealing to read poems in which is presented another, and peculiarly Chinese, attitude toward the world, its attractions and delights. We shall read in Chapter 7 poems with a Taoist drift. If the Taoist places a highest value on *diem*, he downright animadverts on *carpe*. The universal *carpe diem* attitude, familiar to Westerners, offers many and many a contrast to the extremely Chinese Taoistic attitude.

CHAPTER 7

Taoism

OF all Chinese ideas, the Taoist ideas and idea of "Tao" seem to perplex the Western reader most. A colleague one day asked me to loan him a Taoist painting to show his "Religion-1" students. He had given up trying verbally to communicate with them on Taoism. "I try to explain Taoism to them," he said, "but all they want to talk about is nihilism." Lao-tzu himself says, "The tao you can tao is not the Tao. The name you can name is not the name. Knowers don't speak. Speakers don't know."

I *Taoism and the West*

Westerners also undoubtedly struggle against their own training and heritage to understand Taoism and "the Tao." The basic movement of the Tao—the way it achieves its effect—is through antiaction. This is the opposite of the Protestant ethic and of the Westerner's natural tendency to take direct action to attain what he wants. Because of the transcendental overtones in Taoism, I once gave to a unit on Taoism in my Chinese literature course the title, "The Philosophy of Not Losing Your Cool." The mimeographed worksheets for students came back from the college stenographic service entitled, "The Philosophy of Not Losing Your Goal."

During the past five years, Taoism has gotten mixed up in the Western mind with Hindu mysticism and has often been lumped together with the points of view of Kahlil Gibran, Rabindranath Tagore, and others with which it truly has little affinity and less similarity save that they all are exotic from the American standpoint.

II *Taoism and Drugs*

A recent scholarly article or two has misled some of the very young about Lao-tzu, claiming for Lao-tzu an interest in drugs which, if it preoccupied later cultists, had little interest for Lao-tzu himself. Nothing could be further from Lao-tzu's transcendental cools than "the heads'" evangelism. Cummings is much closer to it—in fact, he is there—when he writes "follow no path."[1] Even the word "transcendental" gives mistaken ideas about the Taoists: they rather ride "in-with" than transcend.[2]

Next to Cummings, Alan Watts has done the best job to bring Taoism and Taoist thought within the Westerner's reach. Watts cleverly has used the Zenmasters, all who apply the Taoist idea, to induce in his reader's mind a state in which the reader may catch on. As for drugs, the Taoist poet Han Shan (T'ang dynasty) had been there thirteen centuries ago: "Tried drugs, but couldn't make Immortal" (Gary Snyder's translation). One might even have translated the line: "It's not by experimentation with drugs that one becomes 'an immortal.'" So Claude Brown has said the jazz masters discovered it to be in Harlem, in the late 1950's: "it seemed as though the guys who felt that drugs had something to do with it didn't make it as musicians. The cats who were still hanging in there were just good jazz musicians."[3] That is a very Taoist paragraph, if you really understand Taoism.

There are in the world *three* really great Taoist paintings. At the Cleveland Museum, there is a small painting of a man watching mist rise—a little man, sitting with his hands out behind him, in the lower left corner, and then a puff or two of mist in the upper right-hand corner. The rest of the painting is empty space. At Daitokuji in Kyoto, there is the famous "Five Persimmons", which has been often reproduced. And at the Temple of the Dragon's Repose ("Ryoanji") in Kyoto, there is a monk sewing, painted on a screen. Sewing—no one *sews* the way that monk is *sewing*.

III   *Lao-Tzu and Chuang-Tzu*

We can find the Taoist attitude in poems from *The Book of Songs*. The classics on Taoism are Lao-tzu's *Tao Te Ching* and *Chuang-tzu's Book*. The Chinese themselves usually call Taoism "Lao-Chuang philosophy," or the philosophy of Lao-tzu and of Chuang-tzu.

Lao-tzu was born in Southern China around 570 B.C. He served as Keeper of Royal Archives under the Eastern Chou dynasty rulers. Some authorities claim that he met Confucius between 518 and 511 B.C. We do not know when Lao-tzu died. His name in Chinese means "The Old Guy." His book *Tao Te Ching* is about "The Tao and its Energy."

Chuang-tzu lived from 365-290 B.C. His home was in the state of Sung, and descendants of the old Shang-yin dynasty rulers still lived as princes in Sung. Unlike the Southerner Lao-tzu, Chuang-tzu was born well within the area of orthodox Chinese culture. He held a post as minor clerk in his native district. His writings come down to us in a work called simply *Chuang-tzu's Book*. His name means "the Serene One," or "the Calm One"—or, one could say, "Mr. Cool."

IV   Wu-wei

We may find in *The Book of Songs* three of the most important Taoist ideas, or attitudes. I suppose that the most important of all is *wu-wei*, or antiaction. The Tao's effect is called *te*, whence the title *Tao Te Ching*; literally, "Classic on the Tao and Its Energy." The energy operates by antiaction, *wu-wei*. Right away we begin to get into trouble. How do we understand *wu-wei*? Most Occidental writers take it as being virtually synonymous with catatonia. It is scarcely accurate so to take it. *Wu-wei* is not nonaction, it is antiaction. Here is Lao-tzu on *wu-wei*:

What you want to shrink, you first must stretch. What you want to enervate, you first must energize.—What you want to lay low, you first must set up; what you want to grab, you first must give. This I would call a subtle light: the tender and weak overcomes the hard and strong.

Acting, anti-act; working, anti-work; tasting, anti-taste. Magnify the minima, multiply the dividua. Respond to grief with joy. Prepare for the difficult in the easy. Deal with the big in the small. Difficult undertakings must be done in the easy, and great undertakings must be done in the small. Therefore the sage never strives for the great, and thereby he is able to achieve this "great."[4]

Lao-tzu, Taoism do have an attitude against busy-ness. We find this attitude beautifully expressed in "Ole Brer Rabbit Watchin' His Feet" (no. 70):

Ole Brer Rabbit Watchin' His Feet

Ole Brer Rabbit watchin' his feet,
Rabbit net's got the pheasant beat.
I began life with too much élan,
Troubles come to a bustling man.
    "Down Oh, and give me a bed!"

Ole Brer Rabbit watchin' his feet,
Pheasant's caught in the rabbit trap.
I began life with a flip and a flap
Then I met trouble?
    Aye, my son;
    Wish I could sleep till life is done.

Ole Brer Rabbit watchin' his feet,
Rabbit net's got the pheasant beat.
A youngster was always rushin' round,
Troubles crush me to the ground.
    Wish I could sleep and not hear a sound.[5]

The Taoists have this attitude, I believe, because they see that
the Sergeant of the Lawe is typical of mankind: "Nowher so bisy
a man as he ther nas,/ And yet he semed bisier than he was"
(Chaucer). Typical of mankind, or of "manunkind" as Cummings has it: "Pity this busy monster, manunkind,/ not."[6] We
find this dislike of busy-ness again in poem 206:

Let the Great Cart alone,
'ware dust.
Think not on sorrows
lest thy heart rust.

Push no great cart
lest dust enflame thine eye,
brood not on sorrows
lest joy pass by.

Push not the great wheel-spoke
in moil and sweat
lest thou make thy troubles
heavier yet.

The Taoists believe in such action as flows with the natural
process. Chuang-tzu says this:

So some people say the natural holds on within, and the artificial holds on without, and *te* inheres in the natural. Know how nature moves and how man moves, take nature as your basis and *te* as your "still point," and you may without anxiety proceed or recede, shrink or expand: for things return always to essences and to ultimates.

This all harmonizes with Cummings's "A world of made/ is not a world of born." I don't know if it leads us to Dr. Timothy Leary's position that "we must put all the metals back in the ground."

The Taoists believe that what is needed, for an individual to escape from this whirl of busy-ness, is for him to see the world in a different way, and all weird Zen teaching techniques are designed to bring, or shock, the pupil into this new awareness. That is what the "next door" means in Cummings's "listen: there's a hell of a good universe next door; let's go."

V   Sennin

When a man achieved the awareness, or when he was still searching for it, he might bug out of the whole mainstream of human activity and social life, and retreat to the mountains. The Chinese name for this person who has gone into the hills is *hsien-jen,* translated as "mountain immortal" or sometimes simply as "immortal." The Chinese character for *hsien* is the "man" character beside the "mountain" character. The term *Sennin* has gotten into English via Japanese (the Japanese pronunciation of *hsien-jen* is "sennin"), I suppose because Ezra Pound used notes from the Japanese to do his first translations into English. Here from *The Book of Songs* is one of the best of all "Sennin poems" (no. 56):

Hut in the Vale

Made his hut in the vale, a tall man stretched out
sleeps, wakes and says: no room for doubt.

Lean-to on torrent's brink, laughter in idleness,
sleeps, wakes and sings; I will move less.

In a hut on a butte, himself his pivot, sleeps,
wakes, sleeps again,
swearing he will not communicate
with other men.

VI *Delight versus Fame*

We have looked into two of the three most important Taoist subjects in *The Book of Songs*: *Wu-wei* and *Sennin*. Let us turn to the third important Taoist subject; we could find it, in Chuang-tzu's sentence "Don't spoil your delight for fame's sake." We can find the idea presented in more detail in the following famous story from *Chuang-Tzu's Book*:

Chuang-tzu was fishing one time in the P'u River. Two ministers came up. They said they were ministers from the King of Ch'u. The King of Ch'u wanted Chuang-tzu to come and run his kingdom for him.

Chuang-tzu sat there and held his fishing pole. He didn't even turn around. And he said to the ministers, "Doesn't your king have a sacred tortoise that's been dead for three thousand years, and doesn't the king keep his tortoise wrapped up and in a box and stored in his ancestral temple?"

"Yes, that's no lie," said the ministers.

And Chuang-tzu said, "This tortoise, is he better off dead and with his bones venerated, or is he better off alive with his tail dragging in the mud?"

And the ministers said, "Better off alive, we suppose, with his tail dragging in the mud."

"Then go away," said Chuang-tzu, "and let me drag my tail in the mud."

We might take the implication of "dead" here to mean that Chuang-tzu did not want political power, for powerful men in China (as everywhere) often lost their lives in power struggles and shifts of power. Later Chinese poets, like Juan Chi, like "The Drunken Eight Immortals" and "The Seven Sages of the Bamboo Grove," embraced Taoism and withdrew from politics in time of political strife and national chaos, in order to save their own necks. But I think Chuang-tzu probably understood "dead" to mean "having sacrificed one's delight" (to fame). Such an understanding accords with the Taoist viewpoint, it accords with Chuang-tzu's own "Of calamities, none is greater than the heart's death." It even, I believe, accords with Lao-tzu's "Of calamities, none is greater than not to know what's enough. Of disasters, none is greater than the urge to acquire. So the only 'enough' that's enough is to know what's enough." Here is a *Book of Songs* poem in which this attitude is expressed (no. 224):

'Neath Thick Willow

'Neath the thick willow 'tis good to lie,
Let the Imperial foot pass by
If he gi' me a low job it would lift me too high.

Better stay 'neath the willow bough
than crush a toe beneath the Imperial car,
if he gave me a lift, it would take me too far.

A bird can circle high over cloud,
a man's mind will lift above the crowd
reaching employ on high above us all
to dwell in deeper misery when he fall.

Although it is reasonable to take *The Book of Songs* as the
repository of Confucian values, emotions, and ideals, we can
see that the anthologist also put in poems to sing the Taoist
heart. And if *the* basic word Tao is never defined in *The Book
of Songs*, neither is it in any of the canonic Taoist writings.

PART II

Style

CHAPTER 8

"The *Poetry Classic*"

THE *Songs* have influenced Chinese poetry age after age, and the poets show, in their style, rather that they loved and lived with *The Songs*, than that they merely read them and accepted their influence.

If we clearly would understand how *The Songs* had this effect, and why, we must dissociate two kinds of Chinese poetry: we must dissociate scholarly poetry from nonscholarly poetry. I already have discussed the Music Bureau and its functions. We may call nonscholarly poetry that poetry which, in ages after *The Songs*, was collected and preserved by the Music Bureau. Some of this poetry, in its verbalism and in its imagery, is very skillful and artistic indeed.[1] But it was written by people whose names we do not know, people who did not belong to the scholarly class that surrounded the emperor, that governed and that administered justice. The scholars, and therefore the scholar-poets, had to pass a series of difficult examinations in order to get their position and to maintain it, and a knowledge of the Confucian classics—including *The Book of Songs*—was the sine qua non for passing these examinations and getting the civil service appointment.

Confucius used *The Songs* in his teaching and urged his pupils to study them: "Confucius said, 'You guys! Why haven't you studied these *Songs?* They'll stir your emotions, they'll sharpen your vision, they'll perfect your manner, and they'll correct your resentments. At home, they'll help you serve your father; and abroad, they'll help you serve your government. They'll also teach you the names of many birds, beasts, flowers, and trees.'" (XVII, 9).

The Western reader might assume that Confucius was using *The Songs* as belles lettres—"poetry, his border of ideas." Confucius probably took them more seriously than that:

One day, Ch'en K'ang asked Confucius's son Po-yü, "Do you ever hear from the maestro anything different or special?"

Po-yü replied, "Not yet. Once he was standing by himself, and I came along in a hurry across the yard. He said, 'Have you studied *The Songs?*' I said, 'Not yet.' And he said, 'If you don't study *The Songs*, you won't be able to use words.'" (XVI, 13)

We cannot really understand Confucius's remark to his son, unless we understand how much stress Confucius laid on the definition of words. Confucians identify this stress as the doctrine of *cheng ming*, and it is perhaps the earliest case on record of cybernetics applied to government:

Tzu-lu said, "The Prince of Wei wants you to help him form a government. What will you do first?"

Confucius said, " 'Will' do? *Must* do: get the names straightened out."

Tzu-lu said, "Are you serious? This is beside the point. Why get them straightened out?"

Confucius said, "As a student, you're a dead loss.

"If a proper man hears about something he doesn't understand, he shows some reserve.

"If the names are not straight, the language will not be precise. If the language is not precise, the work will not get done. If the work does not get done, then rites and music will not spring up. If rites and music do not spring up, then punishments and penalties will not hit the mark. If punishments and penalties do not hit the mark, the populace will not know how to move hand or foot.

"Therefore, when the proper man names a thing, the thing must accord with the word, the word must fit what the thing does. The proper man, in his language, is never careless. N-e-v-e-r." (XIII, 3)

The Analects also has the following passage on *The Book of Songs*: "Confucius said, 'You can gather up in one sentence the whole three hundred poems: "have no twisty thoughts." ' "

As Confucius had advised his students to do, later poets used *The Songs*, if not to study style, at least to acquire it. It is like the use that Dante made of Virgil. We learn from Dante himself that he knew *The Aeneid* by heart: "Ben lo sai tu, che lo sai tutta quanta" (*Inferno* XX, 114). "Vergil," says Goethe, "gilt Dante als Meister Der Rhetorik."[2] Likewise, all later Chinese poets, except the anonymous folk poets, valued *The Songs* as a textbook of style. So Chinese scholarly poets for centuries wrote of "cloudhair," because of a figure in *The Songs*. Knowing *The Songs* as they did, virtually or actually by heart, later poets found it natural poetically to express themselves with the phrases, figures, and elements of style in *The Songs*. We cannot, then, trace the power and the modes of poetic expression in later Chinese poetry until we know how much of it was there in *The Book of Songs*. We shall draw up in the following chapters a partial inventory of that original stock.

Besides his cadence, his verbal music, the poet also has the resource of rhetorical figures. We are going to consider, in the next few chapters, the verbal music and the rhetorical figures of *The Book of Songs*. We shall consider the verbal music in the poets' meters and in the poets' main forms. The rhetorical figures we shall divide as follows: tropes and schemes. Schemes we shall divide into figures of words, figures of thought, and figures of grammar.

CHAPTER 9

Prosody

I The Line

T HE *Four-syllable Meter.* "It is a well-known fact," writes George A. Kennedy, "that the poetry of [*The Book of Songs*] is composed largely in lines of four syllables. . . . We introduc[e] . . . some general statistics. These are unfortunately subject to a slight measure of error. In a few places in [*The Book of Songs*] there is a difference of opinion regarding the exact division of the lines, because of which figures may vary. . . .

Total number of lines in [*The Songs*]	7293
Lines with more or less than four [syllables]	689

The preponderance of the tetrasyllabic line in 91% of the text is impressive."[1]

The Caesura. If we let A,B,C,D, stand for the position of these four syllables in order, and let | stand for the caesura, we then get the following possible forms of the line, assuming that every line has some internal pause: (1) A | B C D; (2) A B | C D; (3) A B C | D. We find that form (2) occurs by far the most frequently; but this should not lead us to assume that no other form occurs. In fact, types (1) and (3) both occur. Type (1) occurs more often than type (3). Type (3) is quite rare. It is so rare that we may eventually conclude that it is used for some special effect. Examples of type (3) lines are "Ch'i hou ye hui" (no. 22) and "Pi cho che chia" (no. 25). The syncopation is extremely marked.

Lines of More or Less Than Four Syllables. "The 'irregular' lines," observes Kennedy, "vary in length from two to eight syllables, with the following distribution":

No. of syllables in line	No. of lines	Percentage of total "irregularity"
2	7	1.0
3	160	23.0
5	397	58.0
6	100	14.0

7   22   3.0
8   3   .5

Regular "Long" and "Short" Lines. What of the lines which
contain more or less than four syllables? Let us first dissociate
two types of irregular lines: (1) lines of which the musical
definition is longer (takes up more measures) or shorter; (2)
lines which are rhythmically irregular but metrically regular.
Kennedy has demonstrated a "test" by which we may distinguish
type (1) irregular lines from type (2) irregular lines: if the
line is matched in other stanzas by a line which is longer as it is,
or shorter as it is, then the line belongs to type (1).[2] Since the
poet clearly intended at this point in each stanza to write a "long"
line or a "short" line, so as to fit his tune, we should not consider
type (1) lines irregular at all. Kennedy also has suggested the
difference between rhythmic irregularity and metrical irregularity.

Irregular Lines. Kennedy's hypothesis, however, is stated in
terms of linguistic features—levels of stress. I propose to revise
Kennedy's explanation in terms of the relation between words
and a tune. The most common type of irregular metrum
(metrical unit) is composed of three (instead of two) syllables.
We then get the following possibilities: (1) one of the syllables
does not affect the meter (this is the possibility that Kennedy
considered); (2) the three syllables combine in meter to equal
two syllables. These two possibilities may seem at first to be
identical, but they are not identical. Where one of the three
syllables has a less important function to play, it may be
ametrical; but where all three syllables play equally important
functions, no syllable logically can be ametrical. We get two
possibilities in the former case: (1) the ametrical syllable, if it
occurs at the very beginning of a line, may be extrametrical;
such an effect, in the usual terminology, is called anacrusis;
(2) if the ametrical syllable occurs within the line, it may be
submetrical, that is, receive so little a portion of the musical
time that it does not affect the meter. This is the case which
Kennedy describes as "combining *ju* and *chih* in one beat."
What of the metrum in which all three syllables play equally
important functions? The three syllables then will be distributed
over two units of musical time; such a phenomenon is familiar
to musicians as "triplets."

How shall we explain lines of two or three syllables? Kennedy
shows that one two-syllable line—one only—is not matched by a

short line in corresponding stanzas (p. 14). Thirty percent of
the three-syllable lines are not matched. The three-syllable line
then must divide into one syllable + two syllables (or two
syllables + one syllable), and the odd syllable will function by
itself as a metrum—that is, will get double its usual value of
musical time: the classical analogy is in a "resolvable breve."
The unmatched two-syllable line (see above) must have two
such one-syllable metra.

We then get the following possibilities: (1) extrametrical
syllable (anacrusis), (2) submetrical syllable, (3) triplets, (4)
bimetrical syllable (resolvable half-metrum).

Proper Names in Meters. To further explain metrically irregular
Songs lines, we must consider the problem of proper names in
verse. Take the five-syllable line: "Chung Shan-fu ming chih"
("Chung Shan-fu illustrates it") (no. 260, stanza 4). We should
analyze the meter of this line so the proper name, "Chung Shan-
fu," gets two metrical units for its three syllables; the name,
that is, forms a triplet. Proper names in poetry often are accom-
modated thus to the meter by allowing them privileges of
occurrence which are not allowed to other classes of utterance.[3]
Shakespeare's use of the name "Coriolanus" also exemplifies this
pinciple. The line from poem 260, then, divides: *Chung Shan-fu*
| *ming chih. Chih* in this case is not submetrical.

Here is another example: "Hou Wen Wang sun tzu, Wen
Wang sun tzu" ("There are Wen Wang's grandsons and sons,
Wen Wang's grandsons and sons") (no. 235, stanza 2).

The meter of line one, here, also is unusual. I should analyze
it in the following way. First, let us cut it into its logical divi-
sions (immediate constituents):[4] *Hou* | *Wen Wang* || *sun* |||
tzu. To have the logical major pause after the first syllable, so
that it is displaced from the metrical pause, is unusual, but we
already have seen lines in which such a cut occurs: the logical
second cut coincides with the metrical major pause, and the
compensation is worked out at this point (at the second cut).
But because the logical major pause occurs after *Hou,* we cannot
well count *Hou Wen Wang* as a triplet. How, then, are we to
resolve the meter? We apply the principle that a proper name
may occur practically without regard to meter. So that *Wen
Wang* in line one takes up only the second half-metrum, and
the meter works out perfectly; but in line two, *Wen Wang*
takes up the first full metrum.

II   *The Distich*

Almost every line in *The Book of Songs* should be self-contained or potentially self-contained, that is, able to stand as a complete sentence. This principle is generally recognized, although I believe that we could use Chou Fa-kao's concept of the "minor sentence"[5] and Wang Nien-sun's work on particles to diminish even more the number of *Book of Songs* lines that have been taken—especially by translators into English—as incomplete syntactic units; for example, noun phrases. My purpose here is to show that the possibility of occurrence of such incomplete units may be further limited.

Principle of Stanza Organization. Stanzas normally are organized from the beginning into two-line groups or distichs, so that the odd-numbered lines of the stanza are distich line-1 and the even-numbered lines are distich line-2.

Occasional tristichs may occur, but they can be distinguished readily because the entire stanza will contain an odd number of lines and will be organized into distichs except for the tristich, which will probably be the last group.

Principle of Distich Organization. Where an incomplete syntactic unit occurs as a verse line, this line will always be distich line-1, that is, will always be an *odd-numbered line within the stanza.*

We can test this theory against a convenient sample of *Book of Songs* incomplete syntactic units. It is a regular feature of Chinese grammar that dependent clauses precede and independent clauses follow. Let us take dependent clauses formed with a common particle: *sui.* We find on p. 226 of the Harvard-Yenching *Shih Ching Index* twenty-four verse lines which contain *sui* and which must, therefore, be dependent clauses. If we check the lines against the poem texts, we find that every one of them occurs as an odd-number line in its stanza.

The distich in *lü-shih* is an important substructure of the eight-line unit and may be classified according to its position and functions within the eight-line unit: the second and third distichs bear the special name "jaw joint" and "neck joint," respectively,[6] and are treated differently with regard to parallel structure than the two "outer distichs" (distichs one and four). The distich in *Book of Songs shih* has importance rather as a structure in itself, of which the important substructures are line-1 and line-2.[7]

We might assume further that complete syntactic units were differentiated prosodically from incomplete syntactic units and that the prosodic difference partially or wholly effected the exclusion of incomplete units from distich line-2. The prosodic feature was sentence-intonation. If we use a dot high after a letter, P· to symbolize the high pitch of sentence nonfinal intonation,[8] and use a dot low after a letter, P. to symbolize the low pitch of sentence final intonation, we can describe as follows the possibilities for *Book of Songs* distichs: P.Q., or P·Q..[9]

III *Rhyme*

"Nearly all the pieces in the collection," says Legge, "are composed in rhyme" (p. 96). The rhyme, naturally, is usually on the last syllable in the line.

But sometimes instead of last syllables, the next-to-last syllables of lines rhyme. As such next-to-last syllable rhyming is a special case, we should look at it briefly. Kennedy writes, "There is a considerable number of lines that rhyme in the penultimate syllable. These lines generally end in *hsi, i, ye, chih,* or some similar element. It is the rule that lines with end-rhymes are associated together, and lines with penultimate rhymes; that is, we do not get cross-rhyming of the third syllable of one four-character line with the fourth syllable of another."

Kennedy assumes that where lines rhyme on the next-to-last syllable, the usual *hsi, i, ye, chih* or whatever on which the line ends, is unstressed. Since these are all grammatical particles, and would be unstressed in ordinary speech, it is a reasonable assumption to make. Kennedy says, "If we . . . represent an unstressed point by *a,* a stressed point by *b,* and rhyming by capitalizing, we may set up two formulae for the two kinds of lines found:

(1) a-b-a-B   (2) b-a-B-a."

Then in "The Songs of Wei," for example, we shall find 402 lines of type (1) and 95 lines of type (2).

Legge further points out that "in all parts of [*The Book of Songs*], there are multitudes of lines, sometimes one, and sometimes more, which do not rhyme with any others, in the same stanza, while in Part IV, Book I, there are at least eight pieces in which there is no attempt at rhyme at all" (p. 100).

Let us look now at the patterns of rhyme which we find. By

far the most common is to have alternate lines rhyme: the Chinese always seem to have favored alternate-line rhyme to couplets. Of alternate-line rhymes, the commonest patterns are *abcb,* and *aaba.* The reader will note, of course, that the first pattern also contains a couplet rhyme.

In the first two stanzas of "The Levees of Ju," the translator has used an *abcb* rhyme scheme (no. 10):

By the Levees of Ju

> By the levees of Ju
> I cut boughs in the brake,
> not seeing milord
> to ease heart-ache.
>
> I have seen him
> by the levees of Ju, 'tis enough,
> cutting the boughs, to know
> he'll not cast me off.
>
> Square fish with a ruddy tail,
> though the king's house blaze, and though
> thou blaze as that house, the faith
> of thy forebears shall not fail.

The translator in "Field Not Too Great a Field" follows the *abcb* pattern throughout, giving him, for the three-stanza poem, the rhyme scheme *abcb, defe, ghih* (no. 102):

Field not too Great a Field

> Field not too great a field
> lest weeds outproud thy grain;
> nor of foreign affairs
> lest 'ou break under strain.
>
> Field not too great a field
> lest the overgrowth break thee,
> nor foreigners
> lest worry unmake thee.
>
> The tufted babe
> that wriggles in thy lap,
> ere thou art ware
> will wear a grown man's cap.

We saw in the third stanza of "Pheasant-cock" the rhyme pattern *aaba* (cf. above, p. 43):

> Look up to the sun and moon
> in my thought the long pain,
> the road is so long, how
> shall I come again

—if we construe as rhyme the accord, or consonance, of "moon" with "pain" and "again."[10]

Other patterns of rhyming frequently occurring in the *Songs* are the patterns *abab, abbb,* and *aaaa.* We also do find some out-and-out couplets, such as *aabbccddeeffgg.* And we can find combinations of the above patterns, such as *abcbdded.*

Of the patterns *abab,* we find an example in the third stanza of the translation of "Bottle-Gourd" (no. 34):

> Bitter the gourd leaf,
> passed the high-water mark,
> "Let the deep drench,
> o'er shallows lift a sark!"
>
> At the over-flooded ford:
> "Won't wet an axle block!"
> Hen pheasant cries,
> seeking her pheasant cock.
>
> Tranquil the wild goose's note
> at sunrise, ere ice gins thaw,
> noble takes mate
> observing the antient law.
>
> Boatman cocks thumb,
> some go,
> I do not so,
> Waiting till my man come.[11]

Of lines rhymed in succession, we find an interesting case in the translator's version of "Plum Flowers So Splendid Be" (no. 24):

> Plum flowers so splendid be,
> rolling, onrolling quietly,
> a royal car with young royalty.

Flowers of plum abundantly,
Heiress of P'ing, heir of Ts'i,
to their wedding right royally.

Tight as strands in fisherman's line
may this pair in love combine,
heir and heiress loyally,
whereby P'ing is bound to Ts'i.

The scheme is *aaa, aaa, bbaa.*

The translation of "Deep, Deep the Dew" gives us an example
of a song in which a mixed rhyme pattern is used (no. 174):

Deep, deep the dew
that will not dry till day;
Drink deep the night,
let none go dry away.

Deep, deep the dew
in the abundant grass;
Beneath this roof
ancestral manes pass.

Dew on willow, dew on thorn;
as sun's head threadeth
each good knight treadeth,
of heart-sight, deed's born aright.

"Fellow-" and "trust-" tree fruit
nor think to do it;
true gentles so
do as they do.[12]

In the translation of "Picking the Green Lu Grass," we find
another example of the mixed rhyme pattern (no. 226):

The morning 's over, and I've picked less
than a handful of green *lu* grass.
My hair 's in a tangle, I'd better go wash.

2

The morning 's over and I have got
less than a skirt-full of indigo, five days to come;
sixth: he comes not.

3

When he wanted to hunt
I cased his bow,
When he'd a-fishing go
I carded his fishing line also.

4

Then folk would stand to watch him pull out
tench or bream, bream or trout.

Having now this picture of *Book of Songs* prosody, we may
go on to look at the main forms in the songs.

CHAPTER 10

Main Forms

KENNEDY gives us this valuable information on the main form of the *Songs*:

"We have now to consider the matter of stanzas in [*The Book of Songs*]. Out of a total of 305 [songs], 284 are divided into stanzas.[1] The 21 undivided pieces all come in the last section of the book, among the sacrificial odes of Shang and Chou. Now it has been universally assumed that the [songs] were sung, and this division into stanzas suggests the repetition of a melody. This obvious conclusion could be strengthened, if necessary, by a consideration of the general internal structure of the stanza. Suffice it to say that scores of the [songs] present features of the following type:

> Stanza A   Lines A1, A2, A3, A4
> Stanza B   Lines B1, B2, B3, B4.

Line A1 is identical with B1, and A3 with B3. Lines A2 and B2 are the same except for the final characters, which set the rhymes for the stanzas. Lines A4 and B4 are quite different. The repetition of key lines is so striking throughout the songs as hardly to leave room for doubt that the successive stanzas in a poem repeat the same melody." (pp. 11-12)

Although it does not perfectly match the formula that Kennedy gives above, "Plantain" gives us an equally good idea of the amount of repetition which occurs in the *Songs* (no. 8):

> Pluck, pluck, pluck
> the thick plantain,
> Here be seeds
> for sturdy men.
>
> Pluck, pick, pluck
> then pluck again.
> Pluck the leaf
> and fill the flap.

91

> Oh pick pluck
> the thick plantain.
> Skirts were made
> to hide the lap.[2]

"If we proceed from the idea of a melody to be sung," writes Kennedy, "the important feature of [a poem] is its total symmetry and not the length of a particular line.... Perfect symmetry of the text as it stands is found in 173 of the [songs], with a distribution that is suggestive. In the first section ["Airs of the States"], representing songs of the people, 75% are textually symmetrical. In the second and third sections ["Courtly Songs"], which are mixed in character, 50% are symmetrical, while in the last section ["Odes of the Temple and Altar"], the proportion is only 5%. It is surely significant that the least textual symmetry is to be found in those pieces that we may view as liturgical chants, and the greatest symmetry in the popular songs" (p. 13).

The shortest poem in *The Book of Songs* is 5 lines; the longest poem is 121 lines. If we classify solely by number of lines in the poem, there are forty-nine different kinds of poems in *The Book of Songs*. The modal length is twelve lines, more poems (fifty-eight) of that length occurring than any other length. The median-length is eighteen lines.

"Drooping Trees" can stand as an example of the modal length (twelve-line) poem (no. 4):

> In the South be drooping trees,
> long the bough, thick the vine,
> Take thy delight,
> my prince, in happy ease.
>
> In the South be drooping boughs
> the wild vine covers,
> that hold delight, delight, good sir,
> for eager lovers.
>
> Close as the vine clamps the trees
> so complete is happiness,
> Good sir, delight delight in ease,
> In the South be drooping trees.

Let us also look at one example of a median-length (eighteen-line) poem. Here is "Red Bows" (no. 175):

Unstrung red bow,
honour's token honour'd guest,
from my heart's sincerity,
bang gong, bang drum
till the noon come,
feast.

Red bow unstrung
for honoured guest
to carry away by my heart's cordiality
bang gong, bang drum
at my right hand
till the noon come.

Red bow unstrung,
case it, my guest.
By my heart's cordiality
bang gong, bang drum
till the noon come,
toast.[3]

We can set up a table to compare the poems in the various sections of the anthology. We may use the median length of poem and the modal length of poem as bases of comparison.

	States	Minor	Major	Odes
median length	12	18-30	54	12
modal length	12	16-18	64	8

Now just to specify the number of lines in a poem does not fully describe the main form: we also must consider whether or not the poem is divided into stanzas, or into strophes, and how. For example, of twelve-line poems, we might have poems of twelve lines without stanzas or strophes; we might have stanzaic poems of two six-line stanzas or three four-line stanzas. Of fourteen-line poems, we might have a poem of fourteen lines without stanzas, and a stanzaic poem of two seven-line stanzas, and a strophic poem of two three-line stanzas and two four-line stanzas. Such forms, in fact, all occur in *The Book of Songs.*

In *The Book of Songs,* there are ninety-four different main forms. Of these ninety-four main forms, fifteen main forms are non-stanzaic, forty-four main forms are stanzaic, and thirty-five are strophic.

Speaking of the entire anthology, we can say that the most

popular main form is the poem that has in it three four-line stanzas: forty-six such poems occur. Here is an example of a poem in this form (no. 12):

> Dove in jay's nest
> to rest,
> she brides
> with an hundred cars.
>
> Dove in jay's nest
> to bide
> to bride
> with an hundred cars.
>
> Dove in jay's nest
> at last
> and the hundred cars
> stand fast.

The second most popular form is the poem of three six-line stanzas, of which twenty-two occur (no. 82 can stand as an example of this form):

> "Cock crow!" she says.
> He says: " 'Tis dark."
> "Up, sir," she says,
> "Up, see, get out
> and shoot the geese
> that be flyin' about."
>
> "You shoot, I cook,
> that is as it should be,
> eat, drink, grow old
> in mutual amity,
> guitars and lutes
> in clear felicity.
>
> I knew you'd come,
> by the girdle stone,
> I to obey
> for the second one.
> Three stones at a girdle be
> Signs of returned felicity."[3]

The third most popular form in *The Songs* is the poem of four four-line stanzas, of which twenty-one occur. This form is

the "favorite form" among the "Minor Courtly Songs," occurring
among them a total of nine times. Here is an example of this
form (no. 32):

> Soft wind from South to find
> what is in the thorn-tree's mind;
> thorn-tree's mind, tender and fair,
> our mother thorned down with care.
>
> South wind on fagot
> that was tree when
> she thought of goodness,
> yet made us not thoughtful men.
>
> Smooth the cool spring of Tsün
> flows to the lower soil,
> seven sons had our mother
> worn hard with toil;
>
> Yellow bird's beauty
> makes good in song,
> seven sons
> do her wrong.

Since the poem of four four-line stanzas is the "Minor Courtly
Songs" form that occurs most frequently, we perhaps should
look at an example of this form from the "Minor Courtly Songs"
(no. 234):

> Yellow, withered all flowers,
> no day without its march,
> who is not alerted?
> Web of agenda over the whole four coigns.
>
> Black dead the flowers,
> no man unpitiable.
> Woe to the levies,
> are we not human?
>
> Rhinos and tigers might do it, drag it out
> over these desolate fields, over the sun-baked waste.
> Woe to the levies,
> morning and evening no rest.
>
> Fox hath his fur,
> he hath shelter in valley grass,
> Going the Chou road,
> our wagons our hearses, we pass.[3]

If we reckon by the various sections of the anthology, we find that in "Airs of the States," the form that occurs most frequently is the poem of three four-line stanzas; in the "Minor Courtly Songs," the form that occurs most frequently is the poem of four four-line stanzas; in the "Major Courtly Songs," the form that occurs most frequently is the poem of eight eight-line stanzas; and in "Odes of the Temple and Altar," the form that occurs most frequently is the non-stanzaic poem of eight lines.

We have just read in this chapter examples of the "favorite form" from "Airs of the States" and from the "Minor Courtly Songs." We read in Chapter 2, "Think to Thine Art," which is in the non-stanzaic eight-line form that occurs most frequently in the *Odes*.

The form that occurs most frequently in the "Major Courtly Songs" is the poem of eight eight-line stanzas. I refrain from quoting an example here because I do not believe any of the extant poems in this form is of much interest to the general Western reader. Like Pope's *Dunciad*, they and the events and persons with whom they deal have been too far removed from us by time and other events for us truly to enjoy reading them.

Of main forms that occur in *The Book of Songs*, the poem of two four-line stanzas also is of special interest, for this is the form that later came to be the "sonnet of Chinese literature"— the *lü-shih*. Here is an example of this form (no. 36):

> Why why? By the Lord Wei,
> For the Lord Wei this misery
> sleeping in dew.
> Never pull through!
>
> Worse, worse! Say that we could
> go home but for his noble blood.
> Sleeping in mud,
> why? why? For Milord Wei.[3]

Poem 85 is another poem in this eight-line form:

> Withered, withered
> at the winds' call,
> Uncles you lead,
> I follow you all;
>
> Withered, withered
> as the wind floats,

>You pipe, my uncles,
>I but follow your notes.[3]

When the later Chinese poet went to *The Book of Songs,* he had plenty to study in the way of verbal music and main form. In fact, it was not until the Sung dynasty, seventeen hundred years later—when Chinese poets collected tunes into compendia of about twelve hundred different main forms—that the Chinese poet had a repertoire of such diversity as this. As to the durability of *The Book of Songs* and its forms, suffice it to say that the national anthem of the Republic of China (founded 1912) is written in a *Book of Songs* meter. The anthem is written in the *Book of Songs* favorite form, three four-line stanzas.

CHAPTER 11

The Composite Image

WE have assumed all along that the minute variation which often occurs from stanza to stanza in certain *Songs* lines, has no other significance than such variation has in folk poetry generally.[1] I feel now that the new elements introduced in the variation often work together poetically to extend the meaning of the poem and that the poets consciously controlled the interaction of these elements. The procedures according to which the old poets activated and controlled these elements may or may not bear on the definition of the traditional poetic terms *fu, pi,* and *hsing.*

The *Book of Songs* poets distributed images artfully in sequence so that the impact of image on image creates a special effect. We could call each such sequence a "composite image." When *any* poem contains more than one image, the images "vibrate" against each other; the "composite image" arises when the images relate first one to another and then relate to the theme through the total effect of their combination. A composite image allows the poet laconically to make a complicated emotional and intellectual statement. The *Songs* poets use a number of metrical and structural devices to control this interaction of images in sequence. To understand how the poets work up an effect, we may study the composite image in its various functions.

I   Time Shift

The *Songs* poets often use the composite image for time shift. The composite image is well suited to effect shifts in time and in *The Songs* may perform a time-shift function more often than any other. The composite image may shift rapidly across a short period of time, or it may shift leisurely across a longer time.

The poet in poem 110 speaks in the persona of a conscript on the march.[2] Each of the three stanzas opens as the conscript attains a prospect; but the geographical feature changes each

98

time to suggest a wilder and more barren terrain, as the army moves out into the wasteland and farther and farther from civilization and home: "I ascend that tree-clad hill .../ I ascend that bare hill .../ I ascend that ridge. ...." The "movement" of these lines is in: tree-clad hill > bare hill > ridge. The detail in the three lines works in a single direction; the context helps to lead our attention.

The poet tells in poem 69 of the coming on of drought and its attendant disaster. Each stanza begins "In the valleys grows the mother-wort." The poet focuses in the next line on the mother-wort to render the drought's slowing growing intensity: "But scorched is it in the drier places .../ But scorched is it where it had become long .../ But scorched is it in the moist places. ...." The drift of these lines is: in the drier places > where it had become long > in the moist places. The composite image here again shifts through a longer period of time. By compressing into three lines the passage of this time, the poet has converted an extended drama into a short poem, intensifying rather than weakening the emotion.

Poem 145 tells of a lady's reaction to the loss of her lover. The poet shifts us through time with the sequence below, which occurs in each stanza after the line "By that marsh slope": "There are sedges and lotus plants .../ There are sedges and lotus fruits .../ There are sedges and lotus flowers. ...." The image moves: plants > fruits > flowers. The combination may suggest a cycle of seasons: summer, fall ..., spring. Their combination may suggest also the sort of affair it was: casual love affairs traditionally begin in the spring. We may infer even that she finished the poem in spring, when the season's return in which the affair began so stimulated her feelings that it provoked poetic expression. The lotuses bear no allegorical or metaphorical relation to the lady's grief: they simply are lotuses, changing as the seasons change. The lady's mental discomfort changes also: "My tears and snivel are flowing/ ... In my heart's core I am grieved/ ... I toss and throw myself down on the pillow" (the last line of each stanza). Her grief passes from manifest grief > silent suffering > real sickness.

In poem 53 a lady watches her lover enter the city, and we follow the progress in rapid, "cinematographic" shifts: "In the suburbs of Sun .../ In the outer city of Sun .../ In the city of Sun. ..."[3] The other composite images in the poem render the progress with more specific detail: "Slenderly rising is the pole with its oxtail flag .../ > falcon flag .../ > feather flag." The sequence reminds one of effects in *Alexander Nevsky*. The remarkable thing about the poem is that it achieves with words a sense of movement as precise and vivid as does the film with moving photographic images. The girl's excitement probably rises as she perceives more accurately the size of the gentleman's entourage, a contemporary status indicator: "Fine horses, he has four of them .../ > five of them .../ > six of them. ..."

II   *Emotional Complex*

The composite image also may define an emotional complex. The composite image serves this function with the special effect that it delays release of the emotion. The modern Imagists presented the image instantaneously to give a "sense of sudden liberation."[4] The delay which the composite image forces into this process gives more energy to the final break when it occurs.

In poem 121, a citizen protests against taxes or *corvée*. Carrion birds settle in on the trees. The poet introduces the birds with an image of their strange, slow wing motion: "Flapping are the wings of the bustards." The sequence develops through the stanzas as follows: "They settle on the bushy oaks .../ They settle on the jujube trees.../ They settle on the mulberry tree...."[5] The human energy diminishes. The carrion birds grow bolder and move in.

III   *Intellectual Complex*

The composite image may particularize a quality which usually we discuss in the abstract.[6] The author of poem 18 writes about avarice, as he watches officials file out of court; on their lamb furs, he sees: "Five many-thread tresses of white silk .../ Five twenty-thread tresses of white silk .../ Five eighty-thread tresses of white silk...."[7] The effect is cumulative rather than instantaneous; the accumulation is on a single point. The poet uses the composite image here to give general significance to "naturalistic" details.

IV   *Transmutation*

The poet may touch a tenuous subject with an "artificial" image, to give the subject body. The poet who wrote poem 6 has the difficult job of defining a bride's personal qualities;[8] he correlates her qualities with the following composite image, which is introduced by the line, "How delicately beautiful is the peach tree": "Brilliant are its flowers .../ Well-set are its fruits .../ Its leaves are luxuriant. ..." She passes by suggestion from bride to mother to administratrix[9] in the development of this image, while the simple simile "lady/peach-tree" alludes only to her bridal loveliness.

Whether the poet works with "naturalistic" or with invented detail, he must select elements which exactly define the total theme to which he has addressed himself in the poem, or which define the necessary aspect or fraction of that theme. The author of poem 52 found details which work together with maximum efficiency to present an ungentle, or ignoble, individual; the "correlative" is introduced by the line "Look at the rat," and the details are: "It has skin .../ It has teeth .../ It has limbs."[10] Any substitution (of eyes or nose, say) would seriously weaken this sequence. The composite image replaces an emotional statement and implies an intellectual attitude, besides giving body to the poet's theme—*manunkind*.

V *Praxis and Pathos*

As the poet can suggest to our minds simple images, so also can he suggest the moving or "dramatic" image. And he can force these suggestive dramatic images to generalize like any composite image.

Poem 96 lifts the image of a personality out of three scraps of conversation. The first line is "The cock has crowed." The lady speaks to her lover, half of each stanza: "The court is full! .../ The court is in full array! .../ It is sweet to lie dreaming with you. ..." We almost may see the lady fall back on her pillow.

Poem 110 (see above) suggests a story. The young draftee thinks back to his home; he imagines in successive stanzas the anxiety which his situation causes to father, mother, brother: "'May he still be able to come, and not remain (there)' .../ 'May he still be able to come, and not be cast away' .../ 'May he still be able to come, and not die'. ..." The sequence keeps tensely in the potential the story which it suggests: (1) the boy fails to get leave[11] or discharge; (2) he becomes separated from his unit; (3) he gets killed in action.

VI *The Poetic Problem*

The poet's "immagini forte, quelle create," according to Quasimodo, "battono sul cuore dell 'uomo più della filosofia e della storia." When T. E. Hulme wrote, "Thought is prior to language and consists in the simultaneous presentation to the mind of two images," he elaborated Remy de Gourmont's statement, "L'idée n'est qu'une image usée." Hulme described the relation of word to image in saying that the ideal reader "sees each word with an image sticking on to it, never as a flat word passed over a board like a counter" (p. 10).

The simile is a simple trick to place one image on top another: "She kept off the arrow's point as a mother brushes a fly from her sleeping child."[12] The metaphor is a subtle trick to do the same thing, although it melts together the images rather than superimposing them:[13] "Les éléphants ... Les éperons de leur poitrail comme des proues de navire fendaient les cohortes; elles refluaient à gros bouillons."[14] The poetic effect arises in each case from the combination of simple images, although the form of the combination differs. Each device does its work, with the context in which the poet places it, to generalize the facts—which, according to T. S. Eliot, "is very nearly the whole business of poetry."

Objects alone, if placed in proper context, can interact to give us a complex but definite idea. The catalogue of a farm sale, handled by Ford Madox Ford, can give us the idea of a personality: "The catalogue of an ironmonger's store is uninteresting as literature because things in it are all classified and thus obvious: the catalogue of a farm sale is more interesting because things in it are contrasted. No one would for long read: Nails, drawn wire, 1/2 inch, per lb ...; nails do.k 3/4 inch, per lb ...; ... But it is often not disagreeable to read desultorily 'Lot 267. Pair rabbit gins. *Lot* 268, Antique powder flask. *Lot* 269, Malay Kris. *Lot* 270, Set of six sporting prints by Herring. *Lot* 271, Silver caudle cup. ...' "[15]

The simile superimposes simple images. The metaphorical word melts them together and carries them in with itself. The composite image displays them in an interrupted sequence. The poetic problem is to get simple images that will produce the effect intended.

VII   *The Technical Problem*

The technical problem has two parts: (1) the poet must force the simple images to generalize; (2) he may help to control the interaction so that it serves precisely his artistic purpose. The poets in *The Songs* use several devices that force the simple images together and control the interaction. We shall look at these devices below.

The poet's primary concern is to compose an image sequence which will serve his theme and purpose. Then he should control the images' emotional and intellectual overtones, so that they accord artistically with his subject. The poet must handle both these problems successfully if he is to achieve the necessary unity.

VIII   *Routine and Irregular Images*

The question of unity may become complicated, if we do not dissociate irregular images from routine images. The routine image bears obviously on the theme. The irregular image relates less obviously to the theme.

The poet celebrates the skill of good soldiers in poem 79, and after the lines "The men of Ch'ing are in P'eng ... Hsiao/ ... Chu," the following routine composite image occurs: "The two *mao* lances have double ornaments .../ The two *mao* lances have pheasant (pennons) .../ They swerve to the left, they draw their weapons to the right. ..."

The poet tells of parting in poem 28; his irregular composite image comes after the line, "The swallows go flying": "Uneven-looking are their wings .../ They straighten their necks, they stretch their necks .../ Falling and rising are their voices. ..." The images combine to suggest dusk, a sorrowful time of day. The swallows fade out, leaving only their voices. They do not fly away since we can still hear them, and they do not "stand for" the traveler. Also, friend has followed friend far out indeed into the country. Journeys presumably did not begin at dusk. The coherence of the poem in no way is weakened by the image's "irregularity." "La clarté n'est pas une qualité essentielle de la poésie," writes Gourmont. "La pureté de forme, au contraire, et cela comprend le rythme et l'harmonie générale du poème, est une qualité essentielle."[16]

IX *Invariable and Random Sequences*

We may dissociate the composite images into those in which
the elements occur in an invariable sequence and those in which
the elements occur in a more or less random sequence. The
composite image in invariable sequence leads up to, or suggests,
the significant point, and to change the sequence is to change
the point or destroy it. The images in a random sequence enfold
the point, and a shift of sequence would not necessarily destroy
the point, although such shift might in some cases weaken the
artistry.

Poem 68 tells of a soldier's separation from his wife. The
line "[Even] stirred waters" precedes the composite sequence:
"Cannot float away firewood that is bundled .../ Cannot float
away thornwood that is bundled .../ Cannot float away willows
that are bundled. ..." The composite image leads us upstream:
the soldier and his unit recede steadily inland and uphill, the
waters are unable to bear successively lighter bundles.

In poem 7, the poet folds the composite image around the
significant activity. The sequence might be varied without harm
to the effect. "We beat down [the pegs of] the hare-net" precedes
the sequence: "We knock them ding! ding! .../ We place it
at the crossing of many runs .../ We place it in the middle of
the forest. ..."

We might diagram as below the difference between invariable
sequences and random sequences, using X for the significant
point:

Invariable: O −⟩ O −⟩ O −⟩ X

Random:

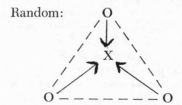

X *Monotonous and Nervous Series*

When the composite image is laid out in any invariable
sequence, the elements may form either a monotonous series
or a nervous series.[17] In poem 63, we may see the images work
in nervous series: "This young person has no skirt .../ This

young person has no girdle .../ This young person has no clothes...."[18] The tension "dips" in the second member of this sequence, so that even more strain is removed to the final statement. If the poet had arranged his sequence "no girdle > no skirt > no clothes," he would have produced a simple crescendo and a monotonous series.

There is no absolute necessity that all the composite elements move in the same direction, although that is the weakest case and probably the most usual. The composite-image poem definitely "rises" with an organic movement; its stanzas do *not* build up like blocks one on top of another; they are not self-contained.

XI *Interaction*

The poet may use verbal similarity to get the elemental lines of his composite image to interact. Or he may set the elemental lines immediately to follow a repetitive refrain and so force them together in the auditor's mind. In the former case, the poet varies one (or two) characters of the line in each new stanza; we already have seen several examples. We may see examples of the latter case—which perhaps we should consider as a refinement, a sophistication of the mechanism—in poem 181, or poem 258, stanzas 1-7.

When the poems received full musical performance, the music too drove together the composite image's separate elements: each element occurs at the same position in each stanza, so that the elemental lines received an identical musical definition. The music drew the composite image more tightly together and defined more clearly the total system of relations within the poem, whether or not the auditor consciously thought about it. The last three stanzas of poem 205 offer excellent example of this effect, in fairly complicated relations. The reader may apply his mind to abstract, from these three stanzas, four sequences which do form composite images; given the music, his ear would pick out the sequences for him without effort.

XII *Traditional Poetics*

Tzu-hsia, or Wei Hung, wrote in his preface to *The Songs*, "So that there are six principles in the *Songs*: *feng, fu, pi, hsing, ya,* and *sung.*" *Feng, Ya,* and *Sung* are the three major subdivisions of the anthology and may be translated as "Airs," "Courtly Songs," and "Odes," respectively. The definition of these terms is not a problem in poetics, nor is the ascription of poems to the categories which the three of them designate a matter of dispute. *Fu, pi,* and *hsing,* however, refer to techniques of poetic composition. *Fu* signifies straightforward statement. *Pi* means "comparison." No precise definition of *hsing* in this context has been transmitted. Mao and whoever collaborated on the Great and Little prefaces, had received a tradition which they didn't quite understand, and the essential dissociations of which they were unable therefore to make with exactitude.[19]

We should not be satisfied with a definition which subjoins *hsing* to *pi.* I would introduce the etymological record of *hsing* and require that any definition accord intelligently with the etymon and its implications. *Hsing* itself as a word appears in about ten different ways in *The Songs* texts.[20] In all of these cases except one, the context suggests an action in several steps or with collective effort, and in several cases the idea of cooperation is engaged firmly. In only one case is there possibly denoted the idea of simple inceptive action.

The *Shuo Wen* says that *hsing* means "to raise . . . , with a common effort." The roots which this dictionary gives for the word mean "in common" and "to lift cooperatively." The latter term is glossed further as a picture of four hands, two apparently pulling, two pushing an object to get it up. Karlgren's study of the bronze inscriptions leads him to reject the "in common" element and read in the picture of a sail. So that he gives the gloss, "four hands and a sail." Nevertheless, *hsing* seems to imply more than merely "to raise"; it seems to imply an increment of association.[21]

Wei Hung was trying to pull together an old tradition, the keepers of which had dispersed when the Chou dynasty broke up. Wei preserved the terminology, but he had lost understanding of how the terms applied, and he was unable to reintegrate with its object the subtlest of them, *hsing.* The composite image has interest to the students of Wei's preface for three reasons, as I see it: (1) the term composite image describes a certain device which the *Songs* poets used, demonstrably; (2) the composite image readily may be dissociated from *fu* and *pi,* of each of which the referent is obvious; (3) if we assume that *nomina consequentiae rerum sunt,* it may be significant that we do not have to force *hsing* after the composite image, the cinematographic analogy of which is called montage.

CHAPTER 12

Tropes

NOWADAYS, people find rhetoric "a pretty scary subject." We have Ernst Robert Curtius's word for it.[1] It's too bad. Without some attention to "rhetoric" and to rhetorical figures, the study of style is a joke.

Confucius says, "The craftsman who wants to perfect his craft, begins by sharpening his tools." The rhetorical figures are some of the poet's basic and most important tools. Unless one can recognize some of them, and see how a few of them work, one cannot begin to understand how a poet gets his effects nor what the bases of his style are. Which is not to say one won't *respond* to them. "The figures," said one astute commentator, "are the sum of all the resources (other than metrical) by which poetry conveys its special overplus of excitement or stimulation; they are the sum . . . of the types of ambiguity, the obliquities, the transferences, the echoes and controlled associations, which lift poetry above mere statement and by which the poet lets odd and unexpected lights into his subject."[2]

The word "trope," as its meaning implies, covers a class of rhetorical figures in which a word is turned from its common meaning to an uncommon meaning. The effect of the trope often depends on the relation between the word's common meaning and the new, uncommon meaning of it in the trope. Aristotle said that one of the tropes—metaphor—is the true index of genius, because the making of a metaphor depends on seeing some similarity in dissimilar objects. Another reason the tropes move one, may be simply that they surprise.

It is usual to say there are nine tropes: metaphor, simile, synecdoche, metonymy, periphrasis, antonomasia, litotes, catachresis, and paronomasia. We will look below at such of these tropes as form an "element of style" in *The Songs*.

I   *Metaphor*

As in most poetries, in *The Book of Songs* metaphor is an important and a powerful trope. The metaphor in Chinese poetry,

107

however, differs from the metaphors of Western poetry in one important respect: in Chinese a good many of the metaphors in poetry, and especially in *The Book of Songs,* are "implied metaphors." We will look at implied metaphors shortly; but let us first look at the more familiar, explicit metaphor.

Explicit Metaphor. We have in poem 34, stanza 1, the line, "Before, nourishing fear, nourishing exhaustion. . . ." The poetess, with her metaphor of feeding fear, of feeding fatigue, more effectively describes the psychological state than she could with any plainer expression. Her metaphor suggests the growth of the fear and of the fatigue, it suggests (by suggesting more usual objects of the verb "to nourish") her efficiencies and her virtues as a wife—an essential point of the poem.

A famous metaphor from *The Book of Songs,* from poem 186, stanza 4, is: "News of you, don't make it gold or jade." "To make gold or jade" here means "to treat as rare, to be stingy about," and the poet at once says what he means and suggests how precious such news is, in fact, to him.

Synaesthesia. Poem 299 gives us the especially interesting metaphor: "His fame glitters, glitters." Of the word here translated as "fame," the basic meaning is "sound," which should make the metaphor even clearer. The metaphor is especially interesting because it is an example of synaesthesia, or trans-sensuous metaphor. We might compare it with Dante's "Dove'l sol tace," or with Pound's "the click of light in the branches," where light becomes sound. In *The Songs* metaphor, of course, sound becomes light.

Implied Metaphor. Most of the "conscious metaphors" in *The Book of Songs*—the metaphors that the poets create to intensify, to clarify the particular subject matter of a particular poem—most of these "poetic metaphors" are, in *The Book of Songs,* implied metaphors. Every metaphor has some comparison in it: call the two things compared, A and B. The Occidental poet then either calls A B, or else he says A does something B does, choosing a verb which is appropriate to B and which is inappropriate— except for his metaphor—to A: "The ship plows the sea," and so on.[3] The Chinese poet makes an even more severe demand on his listener. The Chinese poet just says "B does this or that," and then he starts to talk about A. The reader had better see the connection, had better see the reason the poet had for putting together A and B, had better see it without even the minimal

help he gets from the Occidental poet, or he will miss the whole
point of the metaphor, and probably of the poem. Take for
example poem 233, "Lily Bud Floating," which we read above
(see p. 37). The subject of "Lily Bud Floating" is "the decay
of the house of Chou," and the whole key of the poem is in the
metaphor: lily / house of Chou. The Chinese text identifies the
flower in question as *t'iao,* that is, *Bignonia grandiflora.* The
leaves of the *Bignonia grandiflora,* when about to fall, turn to a
deep yellow. Although the poet nowhere specifically yokes tenor
to vehicle, he makes his context imply the comparison, house
of Chou / *Bignonia grandiflora.* Such is what we mean by
implied metaphor.

"Green Robe" (no. 27) gives us another example of implied
metaphor (see above, p. 25). "Green Robe" has as its subject
that Duke Chuang of Wei took as his favorite son, not his number one wife's son, but a lesser concubine's son. The poem was
written to complain against this. The metaphor is in the robe:
the Chinese consider yellow as one of the five "correct colors"
(the other four are red, blue, black, and white) and consider
green as one of the five "intermediate colors." And they consider
it bad style, and even bad form, to line an intermediate color,
like green, with a "correct" color, like yellow. So that the green
cloth comes to stand for the lesser concubine's son, the yellow
cloth comes to stand for the number one wife's son, and the
"green robe, lined with yellow" becomes a metaphor of the total
situation. The Chinese poets learned early to couch their criticism
and their complaint in such metaphors; this made it less likely
that they would be punished for their perceptiveness, or im-
pertinence. In later ages, this covert critical style came to be
called "the sounds of a dying kingdom," since a lot more such
covert criticism was written when the state was in bad shape.
When things got *really* bad, the government often was so jumpy
it could find this sort of veiled criticism in any poem a man wrote,
and the smart guys stopped writing for publication.

Metaphors in Names of Flora and Fauna. A special subject
for the student of literary style is the metaphor which is "hidden"
in our common name for a flower, a bird, a bug, a beast. This
special subject pretty much has been neglected, East and West,
except for Gourmont's essay in *Esthétique de la Langue Française.*[4] Though writing primarily on French, Gourmont in his
chapters on metaphorical plant and animal names, looks at most

of the other European languages. My opinion is that a study of metaphorical animal and plant names could be made of Chinese, with equal profit. Any language in which the cricket is called "the boss-weaver" (*ts'u-chih*) must have great riches to offer up to such a study. We might also find out why names of flora and fauna so often are disyllabic, where most of the other words in Chinese (especially classical Chinese) are monosyllabic.

Even a cursory look at *The Book of Songs* reveals such expressions as *siog-*siog (a small spider). The characters with which *siog-*siog is written suggest that the two syllables of its name are cognate to the words "embroider" and "silk-stuff," respectively, so that we can (if we want) infer the metaphorical name "the silk-embroiderer."

No doubt a further, fuller study of the early Chinese vocabulary would yield more examples of metaphorical names for bugs, plants, birds, and so on. See also the paragraphs below (Section V) on metonymic names of flora and fauna, and on the onomatopoetic origins of some such metonyms (Chap. 13, Section II).

II *Allegory*

In allegory, the poet carries a metaphor through an entire speech. Hamlet's speech to his mother and Jacques's "All the world's a stage" speech, are famous cases. Everybody's favorite Cummings poem is an allegory. Cummings has had a liking for allegory since he wrote his first book in imitation of *Pilgrim's Progress,* and the success (especially with the young) of this poem proves that as a poetic device, allegory still has great possibilities:

she being Brand

-new;and you
know consequently a
little stiff i was
careful of her and(having

thoroughly oiled the universal
joint tested my gas felt of
her radiator made sure her springs were O.
K.)i went right to it flooded-the-carburetor cranked her

up,slipped the
clutch(and then somehow got into reverse she
kicked what
the hell)next
minute i was back in neutral tried and

again slow-ly;bare,ly nudg. ing(my

lev-er Right-
oh and her gears being in
A1 shape passed
from low through
second-in-to-high like
greasedlightning just as we turned the corner of Divinity

avenue i touched the accelerator and give

her the juice,good

(it
was the first ride and believe i we was
happy to see how nice she acted right up to
the last minute coming back down by the Public
Gardens i slammed on
the
internalexpanding
&
externalcontracting
brakes Bothatonce and

brought allofher tremB
-ling
to a:dead.

stand-
;Still)[5]

In *The Book of Songs,* "Peach-tree Fair" (no. 6) is an allegory. We already read this poem in the chapter on "Love" (see p. 57) and discussed it in Chapter 11 (p. 101). The bride is identified with the peach tree; an implied metaphor is created between the two; and then the metaphor is carried through the second and third stanzas, as the bride (metaphorically, through the peach tree) develops from beautiful girl to mother to mistress of a household. If the metaphor merely were repeated we could not consider the poem to be allegorical; but a definite development occurs, and the development gives us our allegory.

Chinese poetry can give us many many examples of allegory. Later poets, as well as *The Book of Songs* poets, liked this trope. Chu Ch'ing-yü (fl. 825) wrote this poem, which may be the allegorical poem par excellence:

> In their room,
>> the two red candles
>>> are burned out.
>
> Today,
>> she greets his parents
>>> at the great hall.
>
> She makes up
>> her face, and asks
>>> in a low voice,
>
> "My eyebrows,
>> are they painted on
>>> in style, or not?"

Ch'ing-yu sent this poem, with some of his own compositions, to the senior official Chang Chi "of the Water Bureau" on the eve of the government examinations. Ch'ing-yu is asking Chang Chi if his work is of sufficient merit (and, perhaps, if it is of the right fashion, fashion in intellectual effort then and now being as important as in women's dress) to get Ch'ing-yu through the morrow's exams. The allegory is, then: bride / poet; groom / Chang Chi; groom's parents / government examiners; eyebrows / Chu's compositions.[6]

So far, so good. But now, in our study of allegory as a poetical device, we come up against one of the real problems in Chinese literary criticism and in the interpretation of Chinese poetry through the ages. We might call this the problem of the "unwarranted inference": the critic or scholar wrings from the poem an allegorical interpretation which is not in the poem, and which the original poet never intended. I hope that the reader can see by now that though the allegory may seem farfetched to us, the poet sometimes did intend "to mean one thing, while his song said another." That's what makes the problem difficult. Can you imagine trying to explain, to someone removed in time or space from our milieu, the allegorical significance of Cummings's "She being"?

But many commentators and critics, ever nobly desirous of concealing from us the facts of life, take poems of unrequited love, poems of seduction and rejection, poems of delicate and indelicate desire, and say that the poem is not about the ways of men with maids, but really was written by a cabinet minister to his king to say that he should not have been removed from his post. We Occidentals have our exegeticists of the Song of Solomon.

Here is just one example from *The Book of Songs* (no. 67):

What a Man

What a man! with a bamboo flute calls me out
to gad about and be gay
           moreover!

What a man with a feather fan calls me out
to gad about to the stage play
           and then some!

Now of this ditty, the traditional interpretation is: the officers of Chou commiserate upon the disordered and decaying condition of Chou, and they encourage one another to take office, so as to preserve their lives. Chu Hsi held the opinion that it was simply a woman on her man, and we may agree with Chu Hsi. As to the traditional interpretation, well, one can find everywhere in Chinese literary criticism, allegorical inferences fetched equally far.

III Simile

Simile is, as Quintilian tells us, "simply a more leisurely kind of metaphor." The poet uses a word like "like" or "as" explicitly to state his comparison, rather than getting the two elements in with one metaphorical word: "her tiniest invitation/ is like a clock striking in a dark house" (Cummings).

One example from *The Book of Songs* (no. 93) is "There are girls like clouds," and "There are girls like flowers." Many other examples could be adduced. "The Corners of the Ch'i" (no. 55) gives us similes in profusion: "There our prince appears:/ He is like gold, he is like tin,/ Like the sceptre, like the jade." Altogether, the character *ju*—commonest creator of similes in *The Songs*—occurs about 150 times (though not every time does *ju* create a simile), and we can say that simile is one of the commonest tropes in *The Book of Songs*.

IV   *Synecdoche*

The poet may use genus to mean species, species to mean genus, whole to mean part, part to mean whole. In any of these four cases, the trope is synecdoche. Synecdoche occurs often enough in ordinary speech. We say farm hands, and factory hands, when we mean the whole man. A poetic example is: "Where did you go/ Little four-paws" (Cummings).

Poem 219 gives us this example of synecdoche: "For slanderers, there are no limits,/ They destroy the four borders." The word here translated "borders" is *kuo,* "nation, country," but nobody here takes *ssu kuo* to mean "the four countries." The word *kuo* stands, as whole for part, for "borders."

V   *Metonymy*

In metonymy, the poet uses adjunct to mean subject, or subject to mean adjunct, or he uses cause to mean effect, or effect to mean cause. An example of adjunct for subject is: "Doublet and hose ought to show itself courageous to petticoat" (Shakespeare). Of cause for effect: "The moon falls over the portals . . ./ And clings to the walls and the gatetops" (Pound). And of effect for cause: of autumn, "the glory is fallen out of/ the sky" (Cummings).

Poem 260 has in it this metonymy: "Take and bring the king's command,/ King's throat and tongue." The words "throat" and "tongue" are metonymy, as cause for effect, of the king's "words," or "message."

If we studied word families and cognate relationships in early Chinese, we might discover that the names of many flora and fauna are metonymic in origin. Take for example the word **giog,* "owl." The script[7] suggests that **giog* may be cognate to **g'og,* "howl, cry out." We then could suppose that the Chinese who composed and recited *The Book of Songs* thought of the owl as "the hooter"—not an unreasonable supposition. Likewise, the script tell us that *tiǝr* "ram" (male sheep) may be cognate to *tiǝr*, "push, butt," and then the early Chinese called the male sheep metonymically "the butt-er"—just as the Anglo-Saxons called him "ram." See the paragraphs below (Chap. 13, Section II) on the onomatopoetic origin of some of these names.

CHAPTER 13

Paronomasia and Onomatopoeia

GEORGE Kennedy remarked that there are many things we cannot know about onomatopoeia and paronomasia in *The Book of Songs*, until "considerable portions of text are transcribed in accordance with our best knowledge of the sounds represented for that time." But our object here is to get hold of principles, not to make catalogues, and we can very easily get principles on the basis of what we already know. Such is our aim in this chapter.

I *Paronomastic Tropes*

Syllepsis. In what may be a vain effort to bring order into rhetorical study, I have divided the paronomastic tropes into a sylleptic group and an antanaclasis group. The root meaning of syllepsis is "grip together." In sylleptic tropes, the poet does *not* repeat his key word. But in sylleptic tropes, as in all paronomastic tropes, the trope depends for its effect on the possibility of attaching multiple meanings to one word. Several tropes may be classified as sylleptic tropes, but we are going to look at one only in *The Book of Songs*: enigma.

Enigma (or *synoeciosis*). The poet, in the trope enigma, puts together two statements which seem to contradict each other. If we logically analyzed examples, we would see that we could resolve the apparent contradiction by giving two meanings to one of the crucial words. Shakespeare has the famous example "I must be cruel, only to be kind."

Here is a *Book of Songs* enigma: "Hui jan k'en lai, Mo wang mo lai" ("kindly you might have come, /And neither go nor come") (no. 30, stanza 2). Karlgren does not like the enigma of "Mo wang mo lai" and glosses it, "You do not frequent." Waley accepts, perhaps enjoys, the enigma: "Yet neither came nor went away" (p. 93). One can compare to "Mo wang mo lai" Pound's line "She now writes to me from a convent ... /Her ambition is vague and indefinite,/She will neither stay in, nor come out."

We find such rhetorical effects in later poetry, too. Verbs of antagonistic sense are joined in the *Li Sao* lines "Fen tsung-tsung ch'i li ho hsi, Pan lu li ch'i shang hsia" ("Mixed, helter-skelter, they part and join!/The glittering train parting, they rise and fall"). Similar rhetorical effects occur elsewhere in the *Li Sao*: "Ning k'o ssu i liu wang" ("Wherein I die I shall evade dissolution"). Hawkes twists the sense so as to *avoid* the rhetorical figure.[1] (Cf. no. 265, stanza 1.)

The main thing is to recognize what is going on, to see that the contradiction is an essential part of the meaning, to see that the poet *meant it that way*. I can imagine some translator of Shakespeare, centuries hence, annotating to explain that "I must be cruel, only to be kind" "doesn't make sense," and translating Hamlet's speech into "I must be cruel, in order to be harsh."

Surely if the translators and commentators—of *Li Sao* or the *The Book of Songs*—had even a nodding acquaintance with rhetoric and rhetorical theory, they would not be troubled in the least by such passages. They would not try to cast everything into the idiom of the research paper (which naturally does not consist of enigma, synoeciosis or elaborate rhetoric).[2] Such at least is one of the benefits which would come from a greater attention to rhetoric and to rhetorical deviations. Ernst Robert Curtius saw how serious was the loss of classical learning, and the loss of understanding of rhetoric: "Ein neuer Abbau beginnt im 19. Jahrhundert und hat im 20. Jahrhundert Katastrophenform angennomen" ("Things began to slide back again in the nineteenth century, and in the twentieth, have begun to look like a disaster").[3]

The Antanaclasis Group. The root-meaning of antanaclasis is "bend back." In this group of tropes, the poet repeats his key word. That is, instead of all hanging on one word as it does in the syllepsis group, the effect of antanaclastic tropes hangs in two words.

Antanaclasis. In antanaclasis, the poet repeats a word so that the word changes meaning. For example, Pistol says: "I'll steal to England, ant there I'll steal" (Shakespeare). A most famous modern example is Pound's "*tin andra, tin heroa, tina theov,*/ what god, man or hero/ shall I place a tin wreath upon." This is pretty complicated, of course, because it is bi-lingual (and if one pronounced Greek properly, it would belong below with "antanaclastic puns").

The Songs have: "Yun wen Wen Wang" ("He was truly elegant, the 'Elegant King'") (no. 285). The practice of simply trans-literating the sovereign's designations rather loses the flavor of them and can, as it would if we followed the practice here, lead to a loss of poetic effect. Concerning this problem of the actual meaning of titles and designations, consider Majakovskij's remark on *epitheta ornantia*: any adjective in poetry is thereby a poetic epithet, even "great" in *Great Bear* or "big" and "little" in such names of Moscow streets as *Bol'shaja presnaja* and *Malaja Presnaja*. Roman Jakobson says, "In poetry the internal form of a name, that is the semantic load of its constituents, regains its pertinence."[4]

The Songs also have: "Cheng chih shih yü" ("The upright and straight, them He is with") (no. 207, stanza 4). "Hao shih cheng chih" ("The beloved, them He sets upright and straight") (no. 207, stanza 5). I take it that the poet is playing on two ways of taking the image of uprightness and straightness: in stanza 4, the poet says that those who are (morally) upright and straight have God (or the people) on their side; in stanza 5, the poet says that those whom (or that which) God (or the people) love, will be set upright and maintained (will not be knocked down and destroyed).

Diaphora. The trope diaphora, like the trope ploce below, depends on the fact that a word may stand for its referent, or may stand for the referent's nature. Saint Thomas and the Scholastic logicians distinguished between these two uses of a word: "A term put as the subject holds (tenetur) materially, *i.e.* (stands) for the suppositum; but put as predicate it holds formally, *i.e.* (stands) for the nature signified" (*Sum. theol.* III 16, 7 and 4.)[5] Where an iterated word "holds materially" in occurrence one and "holds formally" in occurrence two, the word forms either the trope diaphora or the trope ploce. If the repeated word was a *common* noun, rhetoricians called the scheme diaphora; if the repeated word was a proper noun, they called the scheme ploce.[6]

Take the following line from *Othello*; Desdemona is describing the change in Othello's behavior: "My lord is not my lord."

The common-noun phrase "my lord" holds materially in occurrence one and formally in occurrence two.[7] We have the famous Confucian passage, "Chün chün, ch'en ch'en, fu fu, tzu, tzu"[8] (*Analects*, XII, xi). The four statements perfectly exemplify diaphora. Each of the four words in its first occurrence stands for a suppositum, and in its second occurrence for the nature signified. We can find this rhetorical scheme also in modern Chinese; for example, in such an expression as "Shih-shih shih shih-shih" ("Facts are facts"). The Chinese, in fact, like to use this trope in their conversation. They are using diaphora now to sell motorcycles on Taiwan: one of the favorite current advertising tags is, "Ch'iang, chiu shih ch'iang" ("Power is just *power*").

Take this *Book of Songs* line: "Chin hsi ho hsi" ("This night is some night!") (no. 118, stanza 1-3). I would translate like this because it fits the context, and because the indefinite and interrogative can be identical in Chinese. Karlgren and Legge both give the line this force in their versions. Waley interprets it as a run-on line, in which *chin hsi* and *ho hsi* are adverbial expressions of time and stand as alternative possibilities. I think that the line quite clearly does *not* mean, for example, "What night is it, Tuesday or Wednesday?" Waley has been misled, in my opinion, because he did not understand the rhetorical scheme (diaphora) involved. Karlgren and Legge sensed the true meaning, whether they understood the scheme or not.

Another *Songs* example is: "Fei yen wu yen" ("It's wrong that speech should not speak") (no. 220, stanza 5). Legge notes that this line (and the surrounding context) are not easily explained or understood and that "every critic of note has his own method" (p. 399). Translators into English also have had their difficulty with the line. I would divide the line into immediate constituents[9] as follows: *Fei* | *yen* || *wu* ||| *yen*. After the first cut (*Fei*) we get the residual construction *yen wu yen*. I take it that *yen wu yen* is exactly the same construction as occurs later in the Confucian passage cited above, *chün pu chün* (the difference between the subconstruction *wu yen* and *pu chün* depends on the difference between negatives *wu* and *pu*, and we need not resolve this problem here). We get the two sentences: (1) The ruler does not rule, (2) Speech does not speak. The line, then, is at least not any less clear than Eliot's "The word within a word, unable to speak a word."

Here is another *Songs* example of diaphora: "Fei chin ssu chin" ("It's not that now is this now") (no. 290). Waley and Karlgren attempt this line in tortured periphrases.[10] Legge's "It is not now only that there is such a time" is at least clear, but he loses all the rhetorical effect. The study of rhetorical effect and rhetorical system should enable us more frequently to avoid periphrasis and "explanatory translation." I divide this line into immediate constituents in the same way as the preceding example: *Fei | chin || ssu ||| chin.*"

Such expressions evidently tend to confuse or disconcert the commentator and translator of a later generation. They confuse or disconcert, I suppose, because the same speech form so quickly shifts its logical functions: first it signifies a usual referent, then it signifies the attributes or functions proper to the referent. Yet such expressions are inherently no more difficult than "Shih-shih shih shih-shih," or "Chung-kuo-hua chiu shih chung-kuo-hua."[11] I think that few speakers of contemporary Chinese would be disconcerted by either of these sentences.

Note that there is a slight difference of meaning between *fei* in example two and *fei* in example three. In example two, the meaning is: "It is wrong that," that is, contrary to what *ought* to be. In example three, the meaning is "It is wrong that," that is, contrary to fact.

Anthimeria. In rhetorical theory, a scheme is recognized in which one part of speech substitutes for another, as the noun "knee" substitutes for a verb in the Shakespearean lines, "A mile before his tent fall down, and *knee/* Thy way into his mercy" (*Cor.* 5.1.5). Chinese classical poetry often is said to show "fine versatility" with regard to the classification of its words as parts of speech, or the membership of its words in word classes. And something very like the shift in Shakespeare's lines above is said to occur as a regular feature of *style* in Chinese classical poetry.

Do we have any reason to believe that "class shift" should be classified as a rhetorical scheme? As early as the twelfth century, Yang Wan-li (1124-1206) wrote in *Ch'eng-chai shih-hua*, "There are 'filled words' in poetry, but those that use them cleverly may make 'empty words' of them." Tu Fu writes, "The younger generation '*poors*' the ancient custom/ And some men '*anti-quate*' the scrape and bow."[12] Apart from the fact that Yang used "filled words" and "empty words' in different senses than we now use *shih-tzu* and *hsü-tsu,* the interesting thing about this passage is that Yang notices a rhetorical effect ("clever use") in Tu Fu's use of two intransitive ("stative") verbs so that both become transitive ("putative") verbs. Yang furthermore identifies the rhetorical effect explicitly as a case of class shift. Tseng Kuo-fan more recently has discussed "full words used as empty" and "empty words used as full." He gives as examples of "full words as empty": *Ch'un feng feng jen,* "The Spring breeze 'breezes' them"; (b) *Hsia yü yü jen,* "The Summer shower 'showers' them"; (c) *Chieh i i wo,* "They loosen the clothes and clothe me"; (d) *T'ui ssu ssu wo,* "They push the grain and 'grain' me."[13]

Rhetoricians usually remark upon the liveliness of this figure. Sister Joseph writes, "Of all the schemes of grammar . . . , anthimeria is perhaps the most exciting." Alfred Hart says, "The last plays of Shakespeare teem with daringly brilliant metaphors [*sic*] due solely to this use of nouns and adjectives as verbs." Burton Watson perceives that the scheme in classical Chinese contributes to succinctness and condensation in the style. Watson also suggests that the scheme effectuates the anger in Han Yü's "And let them men their men!" (*Yuan tao*).

But statistical studies[14] of *The Book of Songs* show this: "There is a word-class such that the members of it can function in any primary position in the sentence or as the adjunct of any word that functions in a primary position, including the second. This class includes all the words that we usually try to classify as nouns, verbs, and 'adjectives' ('stative verbs'). This, however, is not the only class (and, therefore, it is not a 'non-class')."[15]

We get, *disjunct from this class,* substitutes,[16] connectives, particles and interjections,[17] and negative adverbs. We find that the members of these classes do not shift—except perhaps two instances of interjections as verbs transitive, which may indeed be anthimeria.

If the data suggest no new theory of word class in Archaic Chinese, they show at least that an hypothesis of "rhetorical class-shift" cannot be used to upset the traditional view. The data also indicate very strongly that, although a hypothetical scheme "*tz'u-te pien-hsing*" (shift in word-class) may be useful to teach modern readers, non-Chinese and Chinese alike, to deal with "class 1" words of Archaic and classical Chinese, yet the "scheme" did not form part of the rhetorical system of Archaic Chinese and would not have been recognized as such by a native speaker.

What then of Yang Wan-li's ". . . but those that use full words cleverly, may make empty words of them?" What of Tseng Kuo-fan's discussion of "empty words as full" and "full words as empty"? Wellek and Warren observe that stylistic features of a language, "not 'realized' by those whose native language it is, are constantly taken, by analytically sensitive foreigners, as individual poetic achievements."[18] Chinese was no longer Archaic Chinese by Sung times but was sufficiently different a language that Yang Wan-li, "analytically sensitive," seized upon one of its most striking features as an element of rhetoric; but he really was comparing Archaic (or classical) Chinese in his mind with the language that he spoke.

Obviously, it is silly to speak of nouns used as verbs and of other kinds of class shift where such word classes do not exist in early Chinese. What this means, to the student of Chinese literature, is that some of the famous cases of a rhetorical figure identified as anthimeria, will have to be looked at simply as an ordinary use of language, however extraordinary the translation may seem; and the rest of the famous cases of anthimeria, like Han Yü's "Let them men their men!" will have to be recognized for some other rhetorical figure. The "other rhetorical figure" will probably usually be, as it is for Han Yü's figure, the figure *diaphora*.

Antanaclastic pun. In the antanaclastic pun, the poet picks up a word he has just used and echoes it in another word that sounds almost like it, so that the reader is struck by the felicitous or absurd congruence of the two words. Lady Macbeth says, "If he does bleed,/ I'll gild the faces of the grooms withal,/ For it must seem their guilt."

Poem 138, stanza 2 has the lines "Ch'i ch'i ch'ü ch'i, pi Ch'i chih Chiang" ("Why, if one shall take a mate/ Must it be a Chiang from Ch'i?"). Chiang was the clan-name of the Ch'i-state rulers. *Ch'i* and *Ch'i* would form paregmenon (see Chapter 14) save that *Ch'i* is a proper noun (state name). But *Ch'i* may occur here in syllepsis; that is, the poet is "punning" on it. Definitions: *ch'i*, wife of first rank (equal, mate); *ch'i*, uniform, equal, even.

Poem 236, stanza 4 has the lines "T'ien tso chih ho, tsai Hsia chih yang" ("Heaven makes him a match:/ She is to the Hsia's north"). Karlgren puts *ho* and *hsia* into the same word family. Definitions: *ho*, to join, bring together, unite, accord; *hsia*, accord. But since *Hsia* here is a proper noun, the lines cannot be considered to contain paregmenon unless a pun (unlikely here) is assumed.

Poems 301 and 302 have the lines "Ku yü cheng ch'ang, T'ang sun chih chiang" ("May they look down on our burnt-offerings and grain-offerings./ T'ang's grandsons bring them"). Karlgren puts *cheng* and *t'ang* into the same word family. If *T'ang* the name is connected with *t'ang* the word, and if the meaning of the word still was an active part of the name in Chou times in some such sense as *T'ang* (the Fiery), then the instance here of *cheng* and *T'ang* could be counted an antanaclastic pun. Definitions: *cheng*, to steam; *t'ang*, hot liquid.

II *Onomatopoeia* (i sheng yü)

Onomatopoeia is very much a part of "making" in *The Book of Songs*. George A. Kennedy, who was a native speaker of Chinese, felt that there was a great deal of onomatopoeia in *The Book of Songs* (even though we read them with a "modern" pronunciation), especially in the doublets. Kennedy felt also that "considerable punning" went on with the doublets. As Kennedy himself says, there are many things about both onomatopoeia and paronomasia (sylleptic and antanaclastic) that we cannot know until "considerable portions of text are transcribed . . ." (see above, p. 116). But even now, we can find many good examples of onomatopoeia:

This is from poem 178, stanza 4: "Jung chü t'an t'an, T'an t'an t'un t'un" ("The war chariots were in numbers, numbers,/ Numbers, numbers, rumble, rumble"). These lines, in addition to the onomatopoeia, suggest the long column of chariots in the continued *t'an t'an/ t'an t'an* and then *t'un t'un*. And the use of *t'an t'an* in a link across the major pause, even "imitates" the army's movements (see below, p. 137).

We can see again, in Tu Fu's imitation of these lines, the impact that *The Book of Songs* had on later Chinese poetry and its style. Tu Fu imitated the effect in the opening to his "Ping Ch'e Hsing": "Ch'e lin lin, Ma hsiao hsiao. Hsing jen kung chien ko tsai yao. Yeh niang ch'i tzu tsou hsiang sung. Ch'en ai pu chien Hsien-yang Ch'iao."[19]

Another good example of onomatopoeia occurs in the song
"Drums and Bells" (no. 204, stanza 4): "Ku chung ch'in ch'in,
Ku se ku ch'in" ("Strike bells! *Ch'in! Ch'in!*/ Strike *se,* strike
ch'in"). The reduplicated *ch'in ch'in* in line one is, of course,
onomatopoeia—in Archaic Chinese, **k'iam-*k'iəm.* Now onomatopoeia in European rhetorical terminology meant specifically
such words as *ch'in ch'in*—words which were created "to imitate
a sound or an action." In the lines "Ku chung ch'in ch'in,
Ku se ku ch'in," the poet has used—in addition to the strictly
onomatopoetic *ch'in ch'in*—other words which simultaneously
make a statement and create a "sound background": *ku, chung,
ch'in* (lute). A great part of the effect comes, of course, from
the iteration and reiteration of *ku.* The lines form a very rousing
commencement for the last stanza of this poem about "drums
and bells." For some verse to set beside these as example of the
successful onomatopoetic presentation of the sound of musical
instruments, I can think only of "E come a buon cantor buon
citarista/ Fa seguitar lo guizzo della corda/ In che più di piacer'
lo canto acquista" (*Par.* XX, 142-144). Dante catches in *buon*
and *buon* the chords of the citara, as they follow and support
the singer.[20]

We discussed above certain kinds of metonymic names for
flora and fauna. Another kind of metonymic name for flora and
fauna occurs where some characteristic of the fauna, flora (or
phenomenon) has gotten an onomatopoetic name, and then
this name is used as a metonym for the phenomenon, flora or
fauna: *miao* for cat, *ya* for duck, *huo* for fire.

We can find examples both that imitate an experience and
that "imitate an action."[21] Of onomatopoetic words that imitate
a sound, we might cite the name **siet-*siuet* for cricket. Of
onomatopoetic names that imitate an action, we might cite the
name **biog-*diog* for mayflies (ephemeridae). The characters
for **biog* and **diog* suggest that the syllables of the name
*biog-*diog are cognate to the early Chinese words "to flit" and
"to drift." So that we can see in **biog-*diog* the onomatopoetic
word, *kata mimesin pragmatos,* "flit-drift," and in the name for
mayflies, we can see the metonym "flit-drifters."

CHAPTER 14

Schemes of Words: I

PAUL Valéry deplored years ago that the rhetorical figure no longer was much studied. Valéry felt that "ces figures, si négligées par la critique des modernes, jouent un rôle de première importance" in increasing the very powers of expression themselves of a language.[1]

Let us begin with a definition of the rhetorical figure: a rhetorical figure is a speech form which deviates, for artistic purpose, from the common usage.[2] Traditional theory holds that deviation means the amplification, diminution, reordering, or partial replacement of a common speech form.[3] What do we mean by artistic purpose? The poet may use a figure to emphasize, to imitate, to add variety, to correct his prosody, to reveal his attitude, or simply to surprise or to delight his audience. Any of these may be an artistic purpose. Quintilian refers to rhetorical figures as "gestures of language" (*habitus quidam et quasi gestus*, IX, i, 11). The poet, then, may communicate his feelings about a subject by introducing these figures or gestures into his discourse at any point.

"The Great Preface" to *The Book of Songs* itself calls attention to the analogies of poetry with music and with dance—analogies which perhaps are most evident precisely in the figures, which are poetry's "gestures" and "*attitudes forcées*": " 'Poetry is where volition finds its place: in the heart, it becomes volition; expressed in words, it becomes poetry. Emotion, stirring in the core, takes form in words. The words are not enough, so that with sighs we proclaim it. With sighs to proclaim it is not enough, so that we draw it out and sing it. Suddenly, the hands are dancing to it, and the feet are stepping to it." The figures appeal equally to the ear and to the intellect: they "are nothing but the organization of patterning: this patterning contented the ear[,] and the identification of patterns was a delight to the instructed mind."[4]

I *"The Three Ornaments"*

Traditional Chinese poetics recognizes three different musical devices: *tieh-tzu,* or iterated syllables; *tieh-yun,* or rhyming compounds; and *shuang-sheng,* or alliterative compounds.

Tieh-tzu. Take the first song in the *Confucian Odes:* the "Fish-hawk Ode" (see above, p. 56). It has in it the iterated syllables *Kuan kuan,* the fish-hawk's cry.

Tieh-yun. The "Fish-hawk Ode" has in it the rhyming compound *yao-t'iao,* which means something like "willing-nilling" and is used to describe the bride.

Shuang-sheng. And the "Fish-hawk Ode" has in it the "alliterative compounds" *ts'an tz'u* or "criss-cross" and *chan chuan* or "tossing, turning." The Chinese listener prizes the effects very much, and they are part of the conscious art of the poet.

Maybe the reader has noticed too the figure *Iu-ts'ai Iu-ts'ai.* We shall talk about such figures later in this chapter; it is a rhetorical figure, but it would not be classified as *tieh-tzu* because the repetition is interrupted: *Iu-ts'ai Iu-ts'ai,* not *Iu-Iu ts'ai-ts'ai.*

II *Schemes of Words*

We shall discuss in the rest of this chapter and in the next chapter the rhetorical figures called schemes of words. In a later chapter, we look at figures of thought and figures of grammar.

The schemes of words are all figures of repetition. Let us look at some of the effects which the poet can get with schemes of words.

Emotional Emphasis. The most natural reason to repeat a word is that the thought behind it obsesses us. So that the natural effect of repetition is emotionally to emphasize the word repeated. John Hoskynes writes, "As noe man is sick in thought upon one thing, but for some vehemency or distress, Soe in speech there is noe repetition without importance."[5]

Demetrius, discussing the "forceful" (*deinos*) style, says that ingeniously chosen figures can add greatly to the force. He mentions especially repetition and cites diacope as an example.[6] "If you take away any occurrence," he says, "you lose both the impact and the emotion born of the impact" (*ibid.,* IV, 211-14).

Glamour. Schemes of words also are important as elements of general style, taking style in Ford Madox Ford's sense as "a continuous succession of small surprises." Schemes of words add to the general style what Robert Duncan calls poetic "glamour." Demetrius's analysis of the effect is so good that I give it in full: to state the word once is the ordinary way, "and everything ordinary is trivial, and hence uninteresting" (*ibid.*, II, 60).

Content Amplification. The use of repetition for emotional emphasis is imitative and poetic; its use to amplify content is sophistic and rhetorical. Aristotle notes that because it is necessary often to mention that of which we will say a great deal, the auditor will assume (perhaps fallaciously) that we have said a great deal about that which we often have mentioned.[7]

Clarity. Strictly speaking, clarity should probably be studied as an aspect of good writing rather than of rhetoric or style; but Wellek and Warren hold opinion that, "All devices for securing emphasis *or explicitness* can be classed under stylistics."[8]

Clarity is an important effect of repetition, and the writer's desire to write clearly may often motivate him to repeat a word. Demetrius says, "For the sake of clarity, the same word often must be used twice. Extreme terseness may give more pleasure, but it lacks in clarity. Just as men running past us may be difficult to identify, so may the meaning of a sentence, if the sentence move hurriedly by, be imperfectly understood" (*On Style*, IV, 197).

Mimesis. Perhaps the poet will use repetition to make the words imitate his subject matter. Tu Fu writes: "From the *one* pavilion you see as *one* the country—/ First *meandering* rivers, and then *meandering* hills." The poet has used repetition here to suggest, by "imitation," this Chinese landscape, which stretches into the distance hill behind hill, and stream after stream. T. S. Eliot uses a scheme to imitate in some of his most famous lines: "I am moved by .../ The notion of some infinitely gentle,/ Infinitely suffering thing." "Infinitely ... infinitely": Eliot uses the rhetorical figure to imitate the continuation, the endurance, which the words express. Let us look at examples of the various schemes of words.

III *Epizeuxis*

In epizeuxis, the poet repeats a word with no word between the occurrences. Here are some *Book of Songs* examples. "Tzu tzu sun sun" ("Sons, sons, grandsons, grandsons") (no. 209, stanza 6). This line counts twice, since both *tzu* and *sun* appear in it doubled.[9] The poet clearly used his scheme here to "imitate" the continuance of the family line which is his subject, and which as always in China, is one of the most important of subjects.

"Yu k'o su su" ("Yes, the guest lodges, lodges") (no. 284). The poet in this figure suggests that the "guest," or traveler, extends his visit to this place—as we say in English, "they stayed and stayed." Some commentators, in fact, take the iteration of "lodge" to mean that he stayed twice the usual time. I'm not sure we need be that literal about it.

"Yü tsai tsai tsao" ("The fish are, are in the *tsao*") (no. 221, stanza 1-3). The poet liked the figure so well, once he found it, that he repeated it with another subject: "Wang tsai tsai Hao" ("The King is, is in Hao"). Here, the poet seems to emphasize the verb of existence—"to be." For more information on the reason for emphasizing this existence and for suggesting the continuance of it, see p. 18 for the entire text of the poem, and see pp. 17-18 where the poem and its significance are discussed in greater detail. If we are going to try in English to get the actual effect of this repetition, we might have to translate "The fish were, are, and shall be in the *tsao*," and "The king was, is, and shall be in Hao (his capital)."

IV *Diacope*

Diacope is formed by the repetition of a word with one or a few other words between. A typical instance is "Who makes *desire,* and slays *desire* with shame" (Swinburne). Shakespeare beautifully uses the figure when he has Iago say "Work on,/ My Med'cine, work!" The figure occurs in later Chinese poetry as well as in *The Songs.* Tu Fu writes "After the debacle, who can return home?/ Another *village* replaces the native *village.*" Tu Shen-yen writes "This year, I *travel* and lodge, alone *travel* in Ch'in./ I grieve and think, and look for *Spring,* being not i' *Spring.*"

Here are some examples from *The Book of Songs:*

"Kuei tsai kuei tsai" ("Come back, come back!") (no. 19, stanza 1-3). This line furnishes an excellent example of the use of iterations to imitate emotional excitement or agitation. The poem's subject is separation of lovers or spouses, "an officer's wife sighs for the return of her husband." She concludes each of the three stanzas with this line. "Mo ju Han le, K'ung le Han t'u" ("None is, as Han is, delightful:/ Indeed delightful are the Han lands") (no. 261, stanza 5). No doubt the reason for this repetition is simple enthusiasm: hurrah for the lands of Han! The Chinese always have felt this attachment to place and this enthusiasm for place.

We can find examples of epizeuxis used to imitate, too: "Chih wo t'ao ku, Tsou ku chien chien" ("We set up our tabours and drums,/ Strike the drums boom, boom!") (no. 301). The poet repeats his words to imitate the repeated percussion of the drum. Note that not only is "boom" repeated, but the word "drum" itself—onomatopoetic in Chinese as well as in English—also is repeated. It is the repetition here of the word "drum" which exemplifies epizeuxis (*cf.* p. 124).

Here is another example: "Yu pi fei shun, Tsai fei tsai yang" ("Swift is that flying hawk,/ Now flying now soaring") (no. 183, stanza 2). The poet repeated "flying" so as to imitate the "soar-glide-soar" movement with which birds, and especially big birds like the hawk, rise up into the sky.[10]

Let us look at another *Songs* example: "Chih ch'i kao shan,/ To shan ch'iao yueh" ("Climbed those high hills,/ Ridged hills and higher heights" (no. 296). These lines are especially interesting because the poet has combined several figures to get his effect. We discuss these lines in some detail below (p. 131). For the moment let us note that the poet, by repeating "hill," suggests the continuing rise of the hill range before the climbers.

Where the poet in the lines above uses a repeated word to suggest continuance in space, he uses it in our next example to imitate and suggest continuance in time: "Chao hsi ts'ung shih,/ Wang shih mi ku" ("Morning and evening pursue affairs,/ Royal affairs are never at end") (no. 205, stanza 1). The poet, repeating the word "affairs," suggests the extent to which he is *affairé*: the affairs just drag on and on.

V *Traductio*

The poet may repeat *more than once* the word on which his figure is based. Then the figure is called traductio. The quality of this rhetorical figure does not differ much from the quality of diacope, but the extra repetition may make the effect more intense or more forceful. Of traductio used *to imitate,* we can find in Shakespeare this perfect example: "Tomorrow, and to-

morrow, and tomorrow/ Creeps in this petty pace from day to
day/ To the last syllable of recorded time."

Here is a *Book of Songs* example: "Hsi fang mei jen, Pi mei
jen hsi, Hsi fang chih jen hsi" ("In the West are beautiful girls./
That beautiful girl, heigh!/ Is a Western girl, ho!") (no. 38,
stanza 3). Cf. Bunting's "I'm bound for the city/ ... George.
Here's/ Girls! Girls!" I suppose that the poet repeats his word
here to suggest enthusiasm or excitement, "... but for some
vehemency or distress...."

VI *Paregmenon*

Just as the poet can repeat words to create a special effect,
of emphasis, of ornamentation, or of imitation, so can he repeat
word roots to create special effects. It is customary to call words
that have grown from the same root, cognates; and cognate
relationship always has been exploited by the poets and good
writers to make rhetorical figures. Shakespeare writes, "*Hardness*
ever of *hardiness* was mother" (*Cym.* 3.6.21). Again: "And
Death once *dead*, there's no more *dying* then" (*Son.* 146).
Confucius said, "Wu ch'eng jen chih o che" ("Looks *vicious* to
me, to proclaim another man's *vice*") (*Analects* XVII, 24).
Mo-tzu says, "Sheng chih, wei hsing ye" ("If you're *born* with
it, you call it '*inborn*'") (VI, i, III, 1).[11] If this effect is subtler
than the effects of iterations that we have looked at already,
if it is lower key, the lower-key quality and the subtlety may be
what give these new rhetorical figures their particular grace
and charm.

The authors of early Chinese lexicons and of philosophical
texts like to give definitions in which the defining term is
related graphically to the defined term—that is, in its "phonetic"—
and related etymologically, for example, "Yu wei er k'o wei, wei
chih wei" ("When a thing is awesome, or awful, we speak of
'awe'"). The so-called paronomastic glosses also often involve
paregmenon: *Cheng che, cheng yeh* "'Direct' means 'to correct'";
i yueh i "'To equalize,' we call 'equity.'"[12]

The dictionary definition of this rhetorical figure is: Paregmenon. [*Para*, beside + *ageio* to lead.] In *rhet.*, the employment
of several words having a common origin in the same sentence
(*Century Dictionary*). We may look at some *Book of Songs*
cases of paregmenon. Paregmenon occurs in as many different

forms—with words between, without words between, and so on—
as does simple repetition.[13]

"Yung yueh yung ping" (*"Leaping, loping,* they handle their
weapons") (no. 31, stanza 1). *Yung: diung; yueh: diok.* K. definitions: *yung,* jump; *yueh,* jump, skip, leap. Type T-NG; family
B603-607. The poet seems with his scheme here to be imitating
the liveliness of the scene he describes. He causes the mind and
ear to leap to a recognition of the sound parallels and of the
etymological parallels.

Here is another example: "Ching kung ming shen" (*"Revere,
reverence* the bright spirits") (no. 258, stanza 6) *Kung: kiung;
ching: kiung.* K. definitions: *kung,* respectful; *ching* (awed),
respectful. Type K-NG. family A73-90. In this example, the poet's
reason would seem to be simply to emphasize the idea of
"reverence."

A third example: "Hsueh yu ch'i hsi yü kuang ming" ("Study
those that *shine* ever in *sheer* light") (no. 288). *Hsi: Xiog;
Kuang: Kwâng.* K. definitions: *hsi,* bright; *kuang,* light, brightness. Type K-NB; family A1-19. We might decide here that the
poet again wanted to emphasize his idea—brightness or brilliance
in this case—or else that he wanted some ornamentation at this
spot in his poem. Either motive would be a legitimate poetic
motive.

The *Songs* poets also used paregmenon for more than two
words in succession—they used it to create "etymological traductio," if you like. Here is an especially good example: "Chih
ch'i kao shan, To shan ch'iao yueh" ("Climbed those *high* hills,/
Ridged hills and *higher heights*") (no. 296). *Kao: Kog; ch'iao
giog; yueh: ngok.* K. definitions: *kao,* high; *ch'iao,* high, rising
aloft: *yueh,* mountain, peak. Type K-NG; family A91-114. We
looked at these lines above because they have in them the simple
repetition "hills . . . hills." The poet uses paregmenon and uses
it again, further to suggest the endless rising and receding of
mountains in the range, about the climbing of which he is
writing. Besides "hills" and "hills," the poet uses "high," "higher,"
and "heights." We see the cognates and repetitions rise and
continue, just as the climbers see the peaks before them rise
and run on.

CHAPTER 15

Schemes of Words: II

S O far, we have been studying schemes of simple repetition. The scheme itself may be complex: paregmenon, which is not the repetition of words but of word roots, is not a simple scheme at all. But so far, repetition has been *the* basic element in the rhetorical scheme which we have studied. We want now to look at schemes the basis of which is a little less simple.

The word which occurs first in a sentence, and the word which occurs last, tend to "stand out" more than the words in the middle of the sentence. The first word occurs immediately after a pause, and the last word occurs immediately before a pause. Now the Chinese use the same word for sentence and for verse line, and the lines in *The Book of Songs* almost always are end-stopped, so we may say that the word which occurs first in the verse line, and the word which occurs last, tend to stand out more than words in the middle of the verse line. There are a number of rhetorical schemes that are based in part on this fact—on this additional emphasis which a word receives when it comes first in the line of verse (sentence), or when it comes last. Let us look next at rhetorical schemes belonging to this number.

I *Anaphora*

When the same word occurs as the first word in a couple of consecutive lines, or more, we call the rhetorical scheme anaphora.

Of modern poets, Pound has written one of the most sustained and most effective anaphoric passages:

> Some quick to arm,
> some for adventure,
> some from fear of weakness,
> some from fear of censure,
> some for love of slaughter, in imagination,
> learning later . . .
> some in fear, learning love of slaughter.
> *(Hugh Selwyn Mauberley)*

Here is an example from the songs: "Lu hsi i hsi,/ Lu i huang li" ("Green hey! shirt, ho!/ Green shirt, yellow-lined") (no. 27, stanza 1-2). The iteration of *lu* as the first syllable of each line forms anaphora. As we saw earlier in discussion of this poem (see p. 109), the colors are key to the metaphor, and green is the focus of attention. The poet emphasizes "green" thus by using it in anaphora.

Another example: "Liang fu ch'i shou,/ Liang ts'an ju shou" ("Two yoke-horses are head-to-head,/ Two flank-horses are like hands") (no. 78, stanza 3). The anaphora here, with the two verse lines lined up on the same initial word, nicely "imitates" the action and image presented. The two verse lines are "head-to-head" just as the yoke-horses, or as the flank-horses, which are so even that they resemble a pair of hands laid flat together.

II *Epistrophe*

So much for this figure which uses the first word in the verse line, because the first word stands out. What of the fact that the last word in the verse line also stands out? There also is a rhetorical figure which uses the last word in the verse line: when the same word occurs as the last word in two consecutive verse lines, or more, we call the figure epistrophe. Shakespeare, in this speech of Shylock's, gives us an example of epistrophe: "I'll have my bond! Speak not against my bond!/ I have sworn an oath that I will have my bond!" The second and third occurrences of "bond" exemplify epistrophe. The first and second occurrences of "bond" exemplify diacope, and the three occurrences taken all together exemplify traductio; but right now, we want to watch the two occurrences at the end of the verse line, for they are epistrophe. It *is* interesting to note, in passing, that the poets often get the effect they want by *combining* various rhetorical figures.

Take this example: "Yuan cheng ch'i lü,/ I an ts'u lü" ("And he marshalled his armies/ To drive back the oncoming armies") (no. 241, stanza 5). Karlgren amends line two so as to get a place name instead of an iteration. Waley leaves the line alone but reads *lü* in line two as a place name—located, according to his note, "In eastern Kansu?" (p. 257). I prefer the original text, in which the poet has set army against army.

This is another *Songs* example: "Jih p'i kuo po li,/ Chin ye jih tsu kuo po li" ("One day he increased the state a hundred *li.*/ Now? one day they reduce the state a hundred *li*") (no. 265, stanza 7). The poet here uses his scheme, epistrophe, to bring out the antithesis: increase, reduce. In being thus by epistrophe yoked together, the antithesis, I believe, impresses itself with more force.

It is possible also to find cases of paregmenon used like the schemes anaphora and epistrophe. Here is an example: "Kung shih chi t'iao,/ she fu chi t'ung" ("Bows, arrows have been mated;/ Bowmen have been matched") (no. 179, stanza 5). *T'iao: d'iog; t'ung: d'ung.* K. definition: *t'iao,* join, mix; *t'ung,* join, together. Type T-NG; family B198-202.[1] The scheme here is like epistrophe. It differs from the examples of epistrophe that we already have seen by using cognates at the end of two successive lines, instead of using the same word. It is easy to see why the poet used the scheme here: he "matched" or lined up his cognates at the line ends, just as he was writing about matching and mating of bows, arrows, and bowmen. This particular rhetorical figure offers an excellent example of how the poet can use rhetorical figures for effects which a cinematographer gets by putting music together with his visual image: see Eisenstein's account of the battle scenes for *Alexander Nevsky,* how he and Prokofiev matched *musical* figures up with the soldier's spears in the line.

Next we may look at an example of paregmenon which is like anastrophe: the cognates occur at the beginning of the line: "Shuai li pu yueh,/ Sui shih chi fa" ("Serves the precepts, not overstepping;/ Observes the signs, carrying out in full") (no. 304, stanza 2). *Shuai: siwet;*[2] *sui: dziwəd.* K. definition: *shuai,* to follow (cause to follow), to lead; *sui,* to follow. Type T-N; family F118-128. K. translates the *sui* as an adverb: "then" (or subordinate clause: "following that"). Waley finds the *shuai* and *sui* grammatically equivalent and semantically related, which would give more force to the iteration: "He followed the precepts . . . ,/He obeyed the showings of Heaven . . ." (p. 277).

The poet here uses paregmenon more subtly, perhaps, than in the example just above, of bows matched with bows and arrows mated with arrows. But in the present example, the poet is writing about order and limits, and he has used his rhetorical figure to emphasize the limits and the order of his own composition in verse. Farfetched? Maybe not. Maybe a difference between poetry and prose.

III *Symploce*

The next scheme we look at combines epistrophe and anastrophe: the two (or more) consecutive verse lines have the same first word and the same last word. We will call this rhetorical scheme, for the sake of tradition, symploce. The Tudor rhetorician Henry Peacham gives the following example, from prose—prose, so that the *clause* end and beginning is the important thing, rather than the line beginning and end: "Him would you pardon and acquite by your sentence, whom the Senate hath condemned, whom the people of Rome have condemned, whom all men have condemned." Here, each of the last three clauses begins with the word "whom" and ends with the word "condemned." The paragraph gives a good example of symploce (in fact, gives a good example of symploce repeated).

Here is a famous *Songs* example: "Che fu ch'eng ch'eng/ Che fu ch'ing ch'eng" ("Clever man, raise a city-wall;/ Clever woman, raze a city-wall") (no. 264, stanza 2). I think that the original poet intended with *ch'eng* and *ch'ing* to set his message into an aphoristic form. He may even be quoting a current aphorism.[3] The only difference between line one and line two is in the pair of words *ch'eng/ch'ing*. The Archaic Chinese pronunciation of these words was **dieng* and *k'ieng* or **k'iweng*.[4] The effect in Chinese is more successful, of course, because the two words (*ch'eng/ch'ing*) are not exact homonyms, where English "raise/ raze" are homonyms.

IV *Links*

Occidental and Oriental poets alike have been fond of a rhetorical figure in which the last word of a verse line is repeated as the first word of the next line. Keats made use of the figure in his famous lines "Charm'd magic casements, opening on the foam/ Of perilous seas, in faery lands forlorn./ Forlorn! the very word is like a bell. . . ." Keats links two lines together with the word "forlorn." For this rhetorical figure, the traditional name is anadiplosis, but the Chinese themselves have identified and named the figure, and they call it a "link" or "linked lines." Since this was one of the felicitous moments in the history of rhetorical theory, I propose that we keep the term "link" and eschew the Graeco-English equivalent anadiplosis. Anyone who spends much time studying rhetorical theory will appreciate Rémy de Gourmont's statement, "Les Savants de Molière parlaient Latin; les nôtres, hélas, parlent Grecque."

Take this example of a link from the early Chinese poet Juan Chi (210-263): "Cranes, each following other, fly/ Fly, fly." Juan Chi uses the link "fly/Fly" to imitate the rising, ongoing line of cranes, and he carries the effect further by repeating "fly" once again in the second line.

The poet also may use a phrase to link together two lines. If the poet ends one verse line with two words and picks up the same words to begin the next verse line, the effect is almost exactly the same as if he had used a single word to end the first line and to begin the next line (see below, p. 137).

Of links, the *Songs* give this example: "Chi ssu wo jih,/ Jih yueh yang chih" ("It runs on through our days/Days, months, to October") (no. 169, stanza 1). As the poet links together his lines with anadiplosis, so do the days link with days, stretching into months. He uses the scheme to imitate, to emphasize, the slow succession of tomorrows.

Here is the entire poem, so that you can see how well the particular figure serves the general theme:

The Lone Pear-tree

There's fine fruit on
the lone pear-tree
and no rest for the king's armee.
One day, then another day,
Sun and moon wearin' away,
October now, let a torn heart grieve,
Will they ever get their winter leave?

Lonely pear-tree full of leaves,
Government work, no reprieves,
Heart can break here in the shade,
Will they ever come back from that raid?

I climb the hill north of the town
to get in twigs of *k'i* willows
as the government work goes on.
Hard on the old folks;
"Broken car?"
"Horses foundered?"
"They can't be far."

> They haven't even loaded yet,
> Can't be coming; never get set.
> He hasn't started, he'll never come . . .

A *Songs* poet used anadiplosis in the lines we saw above (p. 123) "The war chariots were in number, numbers,/Numbers, numbers, rumble, rumble" (no. 178, stanza 4). The anadiplosis is an important part of the effect: to imitate the army's movements, to suggest that the army moves forward in wave after wave, as a pause (the line end) follows the passage of one column, and then another column begins to pass. I find it difficult to imagine a more successful combination of effects to render the passing of a great army.

Here is another *Songs* example of anadiplosis: "Ju ch'ü ju hsi,/ Hsi wu yueh i" ("As one might grasp, as one hand-leads,/ Hand-leads, that's all there is to it") (no. 254, stanza 6). The poet here cleverly has used his scheme to lead line one into line two, just as he writes about leading by the hand. I find very amusing this use of anadiplosis.

The poet in the following example uses anadiplosis again to suggest continuance: "I ssu i hsu,/ Hsu ku chih jen" ("Thus they emulate, thus they continue/ Continue from the men of antiquity") (no. 291).

Of examples of anadiplosis used simply for emphasis, rather than mimesis, we may cite the following: "Wu shih wo ling,/ Wo ling wo o" ("They never assembled on our hills/ Our hills or our slopes") (no. 241, stanza 6). "Wu yin wo ch'üan,/ Wo ch'üan wo ch'ih" ("They never drank at our wells/ Our wells or our pools") (no. 241, stanza 6). I take it that this is simple pride at defending the poet's own land from invaders or encroachers. The musical accent might even be shifted further to emphasize the rights of ownership: ". . . our hills/ OUR hills. . . ."

Let us look at a final example in which the poet seems to have used the scheme simply for ornamentation, to surprise or divert his listener: "Yen kuan ch'i ch'i,/ Ch'i ch'i pei pei" ("Look there at his flags:/ His flags flutter; flutter") (no. 299, stanza 1).

We can find in later Chinese poetry many, many examples of anadiplosis or "links," because the scheme continued through the centuries to be a favorite with Chinese poets. Here is one of the "Tzu Yeh songs":

Spring's wind makes a Spring heart.
Idle eyes linger on the hills and trees.
Hills and trees bedazzle with their brilliancies
And mating birds erupt in raucous song.[5]

The T'ang dynasty poet Chin Ch'ang-hsu (tenth century) uses anadiplosis in his famous poem "Spring Grief":

Beat away
        the yellow orioles,
Don't let them
        on the branches sing.
Singing, they will
        disturb the lady's dream:
she cannot, then,
        reach Liao Hsi.

Sometimes the link may link together two stanzas. We saw such a link in the Keats lines cited above. *The Book of Songs* poets also sometimes used links to link stanzas. For example: "Wu mei ch'iu chih./ Ch'iu chih pu te" ("Day and night he sought her,/ Sought her but did not succeed") (no. 1, stanza 2-3).[6]

The later poet Ts'ao Chih (192-232) wrote a whole cycle of poems where he linked many of the poems to the preceding poem; that is, Ts'ao Chih used the same word or phrase as the last word of the one poem and as the first word of the next poem.[7] This figure, of poem linked to poem, the Chinese rhetorician calls, reasonably enough, a "pulley": *lu-lu-t'i*.

In periods of "mannerism"[8] in Chinese poetry, we find poets who play with link iteration and create various artificial patterns. Shen Yueh gives a good example in the poem "I ch'ing ch'ing ho p'an ts'ao": "Everywhere, everywhere, dust covers the bed;/ In mid-heart, she remembers her old lover./ Old lover cannot be remembered./ In mid-night, long she weeps and sighs./ Weeps and sighs, and imagines his face and form;/ She will not say that they are long apart./ Apart, already it has been quite long;/ And to the empty bed is sent a cup of wine."[9]

V *Chain*

Besides the importance of link iteration as a rhetorical scheme in periods of mannerism, link iteration is especially important in the study of Chinese rhetoric because it is the primitive form of chain iteration. Chain iteration may be defined as link iteration continued through three or more lines.[10] There is one example only of it in *The Book of Songs*, but the example in itself deserves special attention as perhaps the first instance in a literary text of this important scheme. *The Book of Songs* example occurs in the *Odes* section, in a poem which is supposed to have been written between 1264 and 1122 B.C.: "Chao yu pi ssu hai,/ Ssu hai lai chia,/ Lai chia ch'i ch'i" ("He made boundaries to the four seas./ From the four seas, they came in homage/ Came in homage in droves, in droves") (no. 303). The poet uses the chain here effectively to suggest the large numbers that came, and perhaps also to suggest the great distances from which some of them came.

Poem 247 has a chain which is broken by the stanzaic division: "P'eng yu yu she,/ She i wei i./ Wei i k'ung shih," ("The friends have helped,/ Helped with respect and good form./ 'Respect' and 'good form' is as it should be").

Chain iteration becomes a rhetorical stock-in-trade for later prose writers. The following example occurs in the *Chung Yung* (XXIII): "Given sincerity, then there is form; form, then there is clarity; clarity, then there is brilliance; brilliance, then there is movement; movement, then there is change; change, then there is transformation." We could give almost any number of examples, for the scheme is, as Gabelentz says, "a favorite stylistic device."[11] The chain, however, is much better suited to the leisurely and extended statements of prose, and to the arguments of philosophical prose. The lyrical poet does not often let his style spread out in this fashion.

VI *Chiasmus*

The rhetorical scheme chiasmus is a criss-cross of words or of linguistic units. The scheme's name comes from the Greek letter χ *chi* which suggests the criss-cross effect. We can see the effect in the last four words of Eliot's line: "The white sails still fly seaward, seaward flying." The chiasmus, in this case, is accompanied by a change of inflection in one of the elements (fly →) flying). In the following example from John Dowland, the chiasmus consists of one element which is a phrase and one element which is a single word: "That now lies sleeping/ Softly, now softly lies/ Sleeping." The elements are "lies sleeping" and "softly."

We can say, I think, that the function of chiasmus is ornamental in each of these examples. Chiasmus, in fact, is one of
the most elegant and ornamental of the rhetorical devices, and
this no doubt accounts for some of its great popularity with poets
generation after generation.

Apart from being ornamental and elegant, chiasmus also is
one of the most effective *imitative* figures. Osip Mandelshtam
writes: "In a slow vortex, it has woven into double wreaths/
heavy and tender roses, roses' heaviness and tenderness." Mandelshtam uses this chiasmus: (heavy and tender) + roses —⟩
roses' + (heaviness and tenderness). We can see where the
imitation is, if we imagine the progress of objects in a vortex.
First we will see them like this:

Then we will see them like this:

In other nonwords: A — B —⟩ B — A.

Viélé-Griffin gives us an even more obvious example in his
"Lament [for Mallarmé]": "Here's a little of us, a soft song/
that turns and falls/ just as these leaves fall and turn." The
chiasmus in "turns and falls" and "fall and turn" imitates exactly
what the words say—a fine example of, not sound but, rhetoric
joined to sense. Here is one *Songs* example: "Tien tao shang i,/
Tao chih tien chih" ("Upside down he turns his clothes,/
Downside up he turns them") (no. 100, stanza 2). The chiasmus
is *tien tao* —⟩ *tao . . . tien.* The mimesis is very successfully
effected. Just as the protagonist, in his haste, twists his clothes
this way and that way trying to get them on properly, so the
poet turns his words around. The poet of poem 100 strengthened

his effect in two additional ways: (1) the two lines given above respond to almost identical lines in stanza 1: "tien tao i shang, tien chih tao chih" (Upside down he turns his clothes, Upside down he turns them"). No chiasmus of *tien tao* occurs here, so that when in stanza two the auditor again hears *tien tao,* he will be prepared to hear it again in the next line; and when it occurs this time, not *tien tao* but *tao tien,* his surprise will be greater. (2) The poet also has worked chiasmus into the line "tien tao i shang"; when this line occurs in stanza two it occurs as "tien tao shang i." The chiasmus is *i shang* —⟩ *shang i.* Now the effect in this case may be weaker, because the lines fall into different stanzas. We should remember two things, however: (1) each line was probably sung to an identical melodic phrase, since they occur at the same position in the stanza (each is the second line in its stanza); (2) the members of societies which are less dependent on the printed or written word than we are, learn better than we do to catch spoken words and to retain them more precisely. I don't think that the *i shang* —⟩ *shang i* effect would have been lost on many members of the original audience for these poems, especially since the effect works together so well with the content. Karlgren, Legge, and Waley all carefully avoid any suggestion of chiasmus in their versions; although Waley almost gets the *i shang . . . shang i* effect, he changes his translation of *i* so that the chiasmus is avoided: "But he bustles into jacket and skirt . . . but he bustles into skirt and coat" (p. 37). Pound gets both effects: "mistaking a kilt for a coat . . . mistaking a coat for a kilt," and "upside down . . . down for up."

A *Songs* poet uses chiasmus nicely in these lines: Hsu Fang i sao,/ Chen ching Hsu fang: "Hsuland was mightily rattled;/ Earthquake-shaken was Hsuland" (no. 263, stanza 3). The form of chiasmus here is subject-predicate/predicate-subject. One line later, we get a line which is chiasmatic of "Chen ching Hsu fang": "Hsu fang chen ching." If we consider this whole sequence, we can see how the poet has used chiasmus to reinforce this content: the land of Hsu is turned around and turned around again: as the real land in a real earthquake would be inverted and re-verted—and as the equanimity of the Hsu populace, according to the poet, was turned over and over as the Son of Heaven mobilized against them: "Hsu fang i sao, Chen ching Hsu fang, Ju lei ju t'ing, Hsu fang chen ching" ("Hsuland was mightily rattled;/ Earthquake-shaken was Hsuland,/ Like thunder-strokes, like thunder-claps,/ Hsuland was earthquake-shaken"). Hsuland goes through the following cycles: Subject-1-predicate-1/ Predicate-2-subject-1/ . . . Subject-1-predicate-2. I would say that this is rhetoric of a very high order.

VII *Antimetabole*

The scheme antimetabole is chiasmus in which the poet turns around a whole sentence. Antimetabole is one of the most effective devices of orator and wit alike. Simonides gives an example: "I don't write poems because the kind of poems I want to write, I can't, and the kind of poems I can write, I don't want to." Shakespeare writes, "Tis a question left us yet to prove,/ Whether love lead fortune, or else fortune love."

The *Songs* have this example of antimetabole: "Pu ssu ch'i fan,/ Fan shih pu ssu" ("I did not think it would change,/ Change—that I did not think") (no. 58, stanza 6). These lines constitute the climax of the poem, and the next line—"And it's all over now, alas."—resolves it. These lines give an especially effective example of the chiasmus: the lines "imitate" simultaneously the utterer's state of mind and the content.[12] The chiasmus "imitates" the lady's state of mind as the mind tries to reconcile an old certitude—"it will last forever"—with an immediate fact. At the same time, the chiasmus suggests—exemplifies[13]—*change*.

None of the *Book of Songs* examples is antithetical. In the antithetical antimetabole, *contrasted* ideas are juxtaposed as the words are transposed, as in the oft-quoted sentence from John F. Kennedy's inaugural address, "Do not ask what your country can do for you: ask what you can do for your country."[14] Perhaps the most famous English example of this rhetorical figure is Shakespeare's "Fair's foul, foul's fair"—which in its topsy-turvy rhetorical structure imitates the turvy-topsy condition of the world, and that's what the poet is talking about.

Although we do not find in *The Book of Songs* any fully developed example of antimetabole, we have seen some chiasmatic figures in which it is all but fully developed. The later Chinese poet did develop it fully, and we find in later Chinese literature the fully developed figure.

Su Shih's famous evaluation of Wang Wei is an example: "shih chung yu hua; hua chung yu shih" ("In his poems are paintings, and in his paintings are poems").[15]

Here, from Fan Yun, is an example of especially effective antimetabole: in fact, Fan makes it carry his whole poem:

Separation

> To the east, to the west
>> of the walls of Lo Yang,
> How many times,
>> we have said goodbye to each other!
> Before, when I left,
>> the snow seemed to be flowers;
> Today, when I come back,
>> the flowers seem to be snow.

The Palace (*Kung-t'ing*) poets and the influential figurist Shang-kuan I evolved an elaborate theory of parallelism, in which two major classifications were produced. The two classifications were the so-called *liu tui* (the six parallelisms) and *pa tui* (the eight parallelisms). The seventh of the eight parallelisms was called *hui-wen-tui*, and it consisted of complex antimetabole. "Ch'ing hsin yin i te, i te chu ch'ing hsin" ("Feelings are renewed, depending as the will is gained;/ The will is gained, following as the feelings are renewed").[16]

CHAPTER 16

Figures of Thought
and Figures of Grammar

ALTHOUGH the figures of thought and figures of grammar are less frequent in occurrence and less dramatic in impact than the tropes and schemes of words, there are two good reasons to study them. In the first place, no study of style is complete without attention to figures of thought and figures of grammar. In the second place, the figures of grammar and figures of thought often serve a special and important purpose in the poet's bag of tricks.

We would err to say that these rare rhetorical figures are less important than the common figures we already have studied. It is a statistical point that the rare figures occur less often than the common figures. We need to know the rare figures and their special uses as well as we know the common figures and their various uses if we are fully to appreciate the style of *Book of Songs* poetry and the poetry itself.

I *Figures of Thought*

Hysteron Proteron. In hysteron proteron, narrating a sequence of events, the poet mentions one event before mentioning another event which preceded it in time. Shakespeare uses hysteron proteron to describe the flight of Cleopatra's ships: "Th' Antoniad, the Egyptian admiral,/ With all their sixty, fly and turn the rudder." They had to turn the rudder, of course, before they could "fly." Shakespeare uses the disordered rhetorical figure to imitate the wild disorder of battle and retreat, retreat and rout, at sea. We might think of Hemingway's heroic colonel, and his remark: "Have you ever *been* in a retreat?"

Here is an example of hysteron proteron from *The Book of Songs*: "Yeh yeh chen tien" ("Flash, flash! Thunderclap, Thunderbolt!") (no. 193, stanza 3). The hysteron proteron here really suggests, rather than that the clap preceded the bolt, that another bolt preceded the clap, and that another clap will succeed to

144

this bolt: that is, a real storm is going on. Let *A* stand for bolt and *B* for clap and suppose that clap succeeds bolt in the process *ABABABAB*. We do not know how long this process will continue, but we do know that it must end with *B*. The poet then, instead of opening the window of his poem on *ABAB[AB]AB* and suggesting that the process might be over, opens the window on *ABA[BA]BAB* and suggests that the process must continue. The effect would be completely lost if the order were *tien chen*.

Dialogismus. The rhetorical figure dialogismus is the framing of a speech suitable to a particular character. Shakespeare so mastered this figure that, using only the words they speak from the stage, he has given us a whole host of archetypal characters: Holofernes for affected diction, Osric for flowery address, Shallow for tedious and inane repetition, Falstaff for bragging. It is Jane Austen's skill with dialogismus that makes her dialogues so easy to follow, whether or not she uses the speaker's name every time.

Insofar as we can know about the speech of 600 B.C., we find dialogismus to form part of the texture in *The Book of Songs*. There are differences between the speech of the "airs," in which the folk speak to the folk; the speech of "The Courtly Songs," in which the aristocrats speak to the aristocrats; and the "Odes of Temple and Altar," in which they speak to the gods.[1]

We also find in *The Book of Songs* incidental effective uses of dialogismus. Take "Shih erh ch'i hsing,/ Shih yeh wang chi" ("Husband, you have doubled your ways;/ Husband, you have no limits") (no. 58, stanza 4). We might well classify as dialogismus the woman's iteration here of *shih*. Another *Shih Ching* example of dialogismus is the *tzu . . . tzu . . . tzu* of the rejected lady in poem 31: she keeps saying to him, "You . . . you . . . you," and we can hear in it her grievance and her grief.

But possibly the best case of all, in which the various characters are differentiated with minimum means, is poem 110: The mother refers to her soldier-son as "My baby," the father refers to him as "My son," and the older brother refers to him as "the kid" (see p. 35).

Emphasis. Emphasis is another important rhetorical figure which, like diaphora, is based on logic. In emphasis, the poet speaks of a substance as if it *itself* was the very quality that inheres in it. Now since many qualities inhere in any substance, which particular quality the poet selects to emphasize, depends

on the situation and his attitude at the moment. Cesario says
to Olivia, "Farewell, fair cruelty." And Prospero says to Caliban:
"Shrug'st thou, malice?" One of the best examples of emphasis
in English is in the anonymous madrigal:

> My love in her attire doth show her wit,
> It doth so well become her;
> For every season she hath dressings fit,
> For Winter, Spring, and Summer,
> No beauty she doth miss
> When all her robes are on:
> But Beauty's self she is
> When all her robes are gone.

Poem 42, stanza 3, has in it an example of emphasis. Naturally,
it is a line which has caused lots of trouble to people trying
to translate it, to edit it, or to annotate it ("Ein neuer Abbau ...").
The example occurs in the second of these three lines: "It is
beautiful and strange./ It is not because of you that you are
beauty—/ Beautiful she is that gave it to me." (see p. 147 for
discussion of the enallage in these lines.)[2]

II *Figures of Grammar*

Let us now turn our attention from figures of thought to
figures of grammar.

Hendiadys. In hendiadys, the poet transforms a modifier +
noun construction into a noun + noun construction. Shakespeare
writes "The heaviness and the guilt within my bosom," instead
of "heavy guilt."

We find in *The Book of Songs* such examples as, from "The
Corners of the Ch'i" (no. 55, "The Songs of Wei,"), "... our
prince/ ... is like the sceptre, like the jade." Legge reads this
as hendiadys of "like the jade sceptre" and translates it so as
to avoid the figure. Another example occurs in poem 255, stanza 6:
"Like the boiling, like the soup." Legge reads this to mean "like
the soup's boiling," but whether you take it to mean "like the
boiling soup," or "like the soup's boiling," it exemplifies hendiadys
of a noun and a modifier. Legge notes that such constructions
as this are "a peculiarity of the ancient poetical style, common
enough in [*The Book of Songs*], and especially in ["The Decade
of T'ang"]" (p. 509).

Aposiopesis. In aposiopesis, the poet or speaker breaks off in the middle of his sentence. Shakespeare uses aposiopesis to give Lear some of his greatest lines:

> I will have revenges on you both
> That all the world shall—I will do such things—
> What they are yet, I know not; but they shall be
> The terrors of the earth! (II, IV, 282)

The songs have this good example: "And beware: Yin from Heaven—/High Heaven does its work" (no. 235, stanza 7). Demetrius's remark is especially pertinent to the figure's effect here: A threat may be greater if it is vague, and more effectively may terrify (II, 99-100). The poet breaks off, does not say exactly what Heaven did to Yin—as if it were too horrible to talk about.

Another example of aposiopesis occurs in poem 47. The poet sings of his lady's features, or of a lady's features, "She has a fair brow,/ Brow that—it is of such hue." Just when he would describe the beauty, words fail him.

Enallage. Enallage is the "deliberate use of one case, person, gender, number, tense or mood for another" (Sister Miriam Joseph, p. 61). When someone does this through ignorance, we call it solecism; but when he does it for special rhetorical effect, we call it enallage. An English example of it occurs in this anonymous song:

> Her gesture, motion, and her smiles
> Her wit, her voice, my heart beguiles,
> Beguiles my heart, I know not why,
> And yet I love her till I die.

"Beguiles" is singular where it would be plural. Cummings among the moderns uses enallage to good purpose. Apart from such phrases as "as for i," Cummings brilliantly uses enallage in his famous

> love being
> you am i are. (73 *Poems*, #31)

The *Book of Songs* poets sometimes use enallage. Here is one example: "It's not that for yourself you are beauty;/ Beautiful she is that gave it to me" (*cf.* above, p. 146). We get a shift of person between the first and second lines here. The poet in line one refers to the flute as "you," and in line two refers to the

flute as "it." Why? Probably for the "gestural implication": singing this, in public, with the lovetoken (flute) as a prop, the
young man looks at the flute and sings the first line—"It's not
that for yourself you are beauty"—then turns and looks at the
girl herself (who is watching him from the audience): "Beautiful
she is that gave it to me."

Here is another song in which we see enallage (no. 186): "Its
man is as jade./ Let not be gold or jade, news of you." The shift
here is from "its" (third person) to "you" (second person).

Zeugma. In the rhetorical figure zeugma, the poet uses one
verb to serve a number of clauses. In English, zeugma makes
the lines sound succinct and sententious: "Our blood to us, this
to our blood is born" (Shakespeare), or "As you on him, Demetrius dote on you" (Shakespeare).

The Book of Songs gives us the following especially good
example of this figure. The poet has used it here for mimesis
(no. 227, stanzas 2-3): "Our footmen, our charioteers,/ Our
divisions, our battalions/ Our march having assembled/ Then,
O! we return home." In order fully to understand this figure and
the effect, we must refer to the principle of distich organization
(see pp. 85-86). These lines violate the principle of distich
organization. Stanzas 2 and 3 achieve their effect, in fact, and
fit the content precisely by virtue of their violation of this
principle. These stanzas describe the marshaling of an army,
and the process of this marshaling is imitated as the nouns
slowly accumulate (without syntactic resolution) in lines one
and two of stanzas 2 and 3, as cited above.

If it is true (as I believe it is) that Chinese poetry deserves
its reputation, that China has produced and nourished as many
great poets as any nation—one German scholar says the Chinese
have written so much poetry it's "scary" (*beangstigend*)—we can
find many of the reasons for it in *The Book of Songs,* and in the
fact that the Chinese *this early* (sixth century B.C.) had such a
foundation for their poetic tradition. Confucius, or whoever else
did it, created this foundation ironically enough by throwing
poems away. But the ones he picked to last, lasted.

Of the reasons for the importance of *The Book of Songs,* we
might select these as especially relevant: (1) the amount of
musical invention in them (ninety-four different main forms);

(2) the rhetorical resources, making of the songs what Virgil for so long was to the West, a textbook of *style*; (3) the tremendous variety in persons, situations, and milieux which we can find in the songs—the variety that leads one to call them "China's epic"; (4) the common history on which they are based: or which, perhaps, they create; (5) the unity of values, social and religious, that runs through all the songs—the unity that has held China together (off and on) for millennia.

China surely is unique among world cultures in the extent to which, at various times in her history, she has turned over the affairs of her state, and the administration of her justice, to men with literary tendencies and to confessed poets. I wonder if that would have happened if Confucius had not laid such emphasis on *The Book of Songs,* and on the study of it?

But perhaps fairly to answer that question, we should revert to our earlier remark that the Chinese aren't Confucian so much as Confucius is Chinese. In any case, the man who will read *The Book of Songs* can see how it all began.

Notes and References

Chapter One

1. Apart from *The Book of Songs,* the "Five Classics" includes *The Book of Documents, The Book of Changes, The Spring and Autumn Annals,* and *The Book of Rites.* Two chapters of *The Book of Rites* later were deemed to be of especial importance and were broken out and studied separately as *The Great Learning* and *The Unwobbling Pivot.* The Chinese themselves call these works the "Five *Ching,*" and when I say "was based on," I mean no more or less than Reischauer and Fairbank mean when they say, "*Ching,* it should be noted, literally means 'warp,' a graphic term for the classic literature that has helped set the pattern and limits of Chinese thought." See Edwin O. Reischauer and John K. Fairbank, *East Asia: The Great Tradition* (Boston: Houghton Mifflin, 1960), pp. 64ff. There was, of course, woof too.

2. The reader will find more on the Music Bureau in "Country Music," in my *Chinese Literature: an Anthology* (to be published by Charles E. Tuttle Co.); and in Lenore Mayhew and William Mc-Naughton, *A Gold Orchid* (Tuttle).

3. The six "lost songs" have left us only their names and their supposed locations within the anthology.

4. See Reischauer and Fairbank, pp. 42-44.

5. For several "songs of Cheng," see Chapter 5.

Chapter Two

1. Ezra Pound, trans., *Confucius: The Great Digest and the Unwobbling Pivot* (New York: New Directions, 1951), p. 19.

2. See below, pp. 79-80.

3. *The Book of Documents* is translated by James Legge in *The Chinese Classics,* Vol. III (Legge calls it "The Shoo King"). Where I give citations for a *Documents* passage, it is to Legge's edition, and according to his system. Scholars now regard some of *The Documents* as inauthentic. We cannot, however, throw out the inauthentic sections, both because we cannot be absolutely convinced by arguments against their authenticity, and because the Chinese for millennia believed the entire text, as translated by Legge, to be authentic. Such scholarly "debunking" has been acutely embarrassed, anyway, within recent memory—as by the discovery of the Shang-Yin "oracle bones."

150

4. In most editions of *The Book of Songs*, the poems have been numbered consecutively from 1-305. As this is the most convenient way to identify a poem, I always will give this serial number when I cite a text. The translations that I give are mostly Ezra Pound's, since his are the only ones from which a reader can get any idea of the literary merit of the originals. Unless a translation of a *Book of Songs* poem is otherwise ascribed, it was made by Pound, *The Classic Anthology* (Cambridge: Harvard, 1954). This book also gives, as a Table of Contents, the best outline of *The Book of Songs*, its parts, and their organization. Other interesting versions of *The Book of Songs*, each with its merits, have been made by Bernhard Karlgren, Arthur Waley, and James Legge. Legge's translations are the least interesting, but his edition—Volume IV in *The Chinese Classics*— puts in the student's hand "critical and exegetical notes," an invaluable "prolegomena," and "copious indexes." Waley's versions are accurate, but his book unfortunately has been arranged in the dullest possible way—according to subjects—and the wise reader will buy two copies, cut the bindings off, and rearrange the poems in their original order. On the problem of Pound's versions, see my "Ezra Pound et la Littérature Chinoise," *L'Herne* IV (1965); "Ezra Pound and Chinese 'Melopoeia,'" *The Texas Quarterly* (Winter, 1967); "Chinese Poetry in Untranslation," *Delos* I (Spring, 1968); and Wai-lim Yip, *Ezra Pound's "Cathay"* (Princeton: Princeton University Press, 1969).

5. My translation: see *Chinese Literature: an Anthology*.

6. See *Chinese Literature: an Anthology* for an illustrative chapter. *Chin P'ing Mei* has been translated by Clement Egerton and Lau She, as *The Golden Lotus*.

7. Duke Sheh said to Confucius, "There are honest men in my village. If a man steals a sheep, his son will fink on him." Confucius said, "There are honest men in my village, too. A father will shield his son, a son his father. There's honesty in that, too" (*Analects* XIII, 18).

8. Burton Watson, *Early Chinese Literature* (New York: Columbia University Press, 1962), pp. 44-45.

9. See below, p. 109 for more discussion of this poem.

10. Pound's version except for the last stanza.

11. Ezra Pound, trans., *Confucius: The Great Digest and the Unwobbling Pivot*, pp. 119-21.

12. In the interests of easy intelligibility, a minor change has been made in the last line of stanza 4, where "unopposed" has been substituted for "non obstat" in the original Pound version.

13. Ssu-ma Ch'ien, "China's greatest historian," author of *Historical Records*, thus was punished for defending a friend and loyalist against slander in the court. Ssu-ma apologizes for not having killed

himself and excuses himself on the grounds that he felt obligated to
finish his father's great work on Chinese history.

Chapter Three

1. Pearl Buck, *The Good Earth* (New York: Pocket Books, 1961),
pp. 121-22.

2. Translated by Rewi Alley, *Selected Poems of Tu Fu* (Peking:
Foreign Language Press, 1962).

3. Since the technique of this "telling the whole story" is fairly
complex, I reserve for our chapters on "style" a treatment of the
poem's technical aspect. A curious reader may want to skip ahead to
pp. 98-106 for this technical discussion. This translation of poem
110 is my own.

4. E. E. Cummings, *Poems 1923-1954* (New York: Harcourt
Brace, 1954), pp. 197-98.

5. The first line in the original Pound version reads: "Pick a
fern, pick a fern, ferns are high." The line has been altered to read
"fern sprouts rise," as being closer to the original and the "dominant
image" of the poem.

6. My translation. See *Chinese Literature: an Anthology.*

7. For more discussion of this poem, see below, p. 109.

8. My translation.

9. My translation. See *Chinese Literature: an Anthology.*

10. My translation.

11. My translation. See *Chinese Literature: an Anthology.*

Chapter Four

1. The Pound version ends with the line, "ripples break no fagot
band," which has been omitted here, since there is no equivalent in
the original Chinese text.

2. More discussion of this poem will be found below, p. 103.
The translation is mine.

3. From Lenore Mayhew and William McNaughton, unpublished
work.

4. *Ibid.*

5. My translation. See *Chinese Literature: an Anthology.*

6. Some changes in wording and punctuation have been made
in the Pound version.

Chapter Five

1. See Arthur Waley, *The Temple* (London: Allen and Unwin,
1923), p. 65.

2. *Iliad*, Book III, 11. 413ff.

3. Based on Gertrude Joerissen's version of Franz Toussaint's version, from *La Flute de Jade*.

4. My translation.

5. My translation.

6. See, for example, *The Golden Lotus*, Chapter 41.

7. Mayhew and McNaughton, *A Gold Orchid*.

8. My translation.

9. My translation. For more discussion of this poem, see below, p. 111. Another good *Book of Songs* epithalamium appears below, pp. 88-89.

10. My translation.

11. Li Po's "The Jewel Stairs' Grievance" is perhaps the most famous later "seraglio poem." Chinese painters also have been fond of life in the seraglio, its anguish and ennui, as a subject.

12. Joseph Needham *et al.*, *Science and Civilisation in China*, Vol. IV, Pt. 2 (Cambridge: Cambridge University Press, 1965). Cited *Saturday Review* (January 1, 1966), pp. 98ff.

13. My translation.

Chapter Six

1. The epigraph is from Pound's "Seven Lakes" canto (Canto XLIX).

2. William Butler Yeats, "Introduction," *The Oxford Book of Modern Verse* (Oxford: Oxford University Press, 1936), p. xxviii.

3. William Carlos Williams, *The Complete Collected Poems* (New York: New Directions, 1938), p. 170.

4. My translation.

5. Mayhew and McNaughton, unpublished work.

6. My translation.

7. Wei T'ai (eleventh century), quoted in A. C. Graham, *Poems of The Late T'ang* (Middlesex: Penguin, 1965), p. 7.

8. Ford Madox Ford, *The March of Literature* (New York: Dial Press, 1938), p. 37.

Chapter Seven

1. Cummings, *Seventy-Three Poems* (New York: Harcourt Brace, 1963), poem 3.

2. Cf. Pound, *Thrones: 96-109 de los cantares* (New York: New Directions, 1959), p. 32.

3. Claude Brown, *Manchild in the Promised Land* (New York: The New American Library, 1965), p. 366.

4. Translations from Lao-tzu and from Chuang-tzu are my own. See my *The Taoist Vision* (Ann Arbor: Univ. of Michigan Press, 1971).

5. This version is taken from Pound's regular and "Aliter" versions. I have done some rearranging, so that the English text shows more clearly the form, and the development of ideas, in the original text.

6. Cummings, *Poems 1923-1954*, p. 397.

Chapter Eight

1. See the Introduction and Appendix to Mayhew and McNaughton, *A Gold Orchid*.

2. See Ernst Robert Curtius, *Gesammelte Aufsätze zur romanischen Philologie* (Bern: Francke, 1960), p. 319. See also Curtius, *Europäische Literatur und Lateinisches Mittelalter* (4th ed., Bern: Francke, 1963), p. 72.

Chapter Nine

1. George A. Kennedy, *Selected Works,* ed. Tien-yi Li (New Haven: Far Eastern Publications, 1964), pp. 10-11.

2. See Kennedy pp. 11-14, esp. p. 13.

3. See Paul Maas, *Greek Metre*, trans. Hugh Lloyd-Jones (London: Oxford University Press, 1962), p. 28.

4. On "immediate constituents," see Rulon Wells, "Immediate Constituents," *Language* XXIII (1947).

5. Chou Fa-kao, *Chung-kuo ku-tai yü-fa* (Taipei: Academia Sinica, 1959, 1961, 1962), 3 vols.

6. The Chinese name for distich two is *han-lien;* for distich three it is *keng-lien.*

7. To the difference here discussed, between distich line-1 and distich line-2, cf. the difference, important for technical discussions of later poetry, between *ch'u-chü* and *tui-chü.*

8. A more detailed, and more technical, discussion of this can be found in my *Shih Ching Rhetoric: Schemes of Words* (Ann Arbor: University Microfilms, 1965), pp. 12-14.

9. Cf. M. K. Rumyantsev, "Some Experimental Data on Sentence-Intonation in Modern Chinese" (in Russian), in *Some Problems in Chinese Grammar,* ed. I. M. Oshanin (Moscow: Akademia Nauk, 1957), pp. 89-127. Relevant parts of Rumyantsev's article are translated in my *Shih Ching Rhetoric.*

10. See the Appendix to Mayhew and McNaughton, *A Gold Orchid.*

11. The arrangement of lines has been revised from the Pound version to illustrate more precisely the original stanzaic structure.

12. This version is made up from Pound's regular and "Aliter" versions.

Chapter Ten

1. I follow the tradition in dividing "Odes" into stanzas, which gives me thirty-four non-stanzaic odes. Cf. *Shih Ching Pai-hua hsin-chieh*, editorial board of Wen-hua t'u-shu kung-szu (Taipei: Wen-hua t'u-shu kung-szu, n.d.). Kennedy is using some other authority, so our statistics on this point do not precisely agree.

2. Based on Pound's version.

3. The line arrangement in the Pound version has been revised to match the stanzaic structure in the original poem.

Chapter Eleven

1. An earlier version of this chapter appeared in *Journal of The American Oriental Society* LXXXIII, i (January-March, 1963).

2. See above, p. 35 for a full translation of this poem.

3. See above, p. 57, for a full translation of this poem.

4. "A Few Don'ts," *Poetry,* March, 1913.

5. Both the size of the trees, and their probable distance from the house, are significant. Mencius mentions the practice of planting mulberry trees close to the house (I, I, iii, 4), and T'ao Ch'ien refers to it in his poetry.

6. A young novelist asked a famous poet, "How can I express the disillusionment of the younger generation?" The poet said, "Their cuffs would begin to fray." Cf. *Ulysses.*

7. For the complete translation of this poem, see above, p. 30.

8. Cf. "Da fragte mich der junge Danner, wie ich das Andante zu machen in Sinn habe? 'Ich will es ganz nach dem Charakter der Mademoiselle Rose machen.' . . . Es ist auch so; wie das Andante, so ist sie." Mozart, *Briefe* (Salzburg, 1865), letter dated December 6, 1777.

9. The last line is "I ch'i chia jen," and the correlation is accurate, botanically.

10. See p. 26-27, above, for the complete text of this poem.

11. Cf. poem 167, "When anyone says 'Return,' the others are full of sorrow,/ Sorrowful minds, sorrow is strong, we are hungry and thirsty./ Our defence is not yet made sure, no one can let his friend return" (Pound's translation from *Cathay*).

12. *Iliad* IV, 129-31.

13. "In totum autem metaphora brevior est similitudo," Quintilian, *Institutio Oratoria* VIII, 6.

14. Flaubert, *Salammbô*. Gourmont cites this passage in his long discussion of metaphor in *Problème du Style* (6th ed., Paris, 1907), p. 90.

15. Ford, *Joseph Conrad: a Personal Remembrance* (London: Duckworth and Co., 1924), p. 198.

16. Gourmont, *Problème du Style*, p. 152.

17. See Eisenstein, "Form and Content: Practice," *The Film Sense*, trans. Jay Leyda (New York: Meridian Books, 1957), pp. 196-201.

18. For the complete poem, see above, p. 62.

19. For a somewhat detailed discussion in English of the "schools" on, and history of, these prefaces, see Legge, *The Chinese Classics*, Vol. IV, pp. 29-33.

20. See my article in *Journal of the American Oriental Society*, cited above, for the details of this argument.

21. Perhaps that is the logic in its derived meaning of "to prosper, to enjoy."

Chapter Twelve

1. "Rhetorik," says Curtius, "auf den modernen Menschen als fratzenhaftes Gespenst wirkt." *Europäische Literatur und Lateinisches Mittelalter*, p. 89.

2. Cited by Sister Miriam Joseph, *Shakespeare's Use of The Arts of Language* (New York: Columbia, 1947), p. 34n.

3. *Cf.* above, p. 102.

4. Gourmont, *Esthétique de la Langue Française* (Paris: Mercure de France, 1955).

5. Cummings, *Poems: 1923-1954*, pp. 178-79.

6. Mayhew and McNaughton, unpublished work.

7. See my *Shih Ching Rhetoric*, pp. 142-43.

Chapter Thirteen

1. David Hawkes, *Ch'u Tz'u: The Songs of the South* (Boston: Beacon, 1962).

2. Various theories exist about the proper approach for a young man with literary aspirations. Ford Madox Ford said, "Let him get a dictionary, and learn the meaning of words." William Carlos Williams said, "Unlearn the language that he learned in the classroom!"

3. Curtius, *Europäische Literatur und Lateinisches Mittelalter*, p. 30.

4. See Roman Jakobson, "Linguistics and Poetics," in Thomas Sebeok, ed., *Style in Language* (Cambridge, Mass.: Technology Press of M.I.T., 1966), pp. 376-77.

5. See I. M. Bocheński, *A History of Formal Logic*, trans. Ivo Thomas (Notre Dame: University of Notre Dame Press, 1961), p. 165.

6. See Sister Miriam Joseph, *op. cit.*, pp. 306 and 84.

7. Chao Tzu-ch'iang has called my attention to the Chinese

poet's line "What is more red than red?" The poet was executed for *lèse majesté* because of the line. The word "red" in its first occurrence here "holds formally" and in its second occurrence "holds materially."

8. "Let the prince prince it, the minister minister, the father father, and the son son."

9. See above, p. 154, n. 4, on "immediate constituents."

10. Karlgren's version of the similar line "Fei ch'ieh yu ch'ieh" is, "It is not that temporarily it occurs for the time being" (!).

11. "Chinese is just *Chinese*." Remark made to me by a Chinese, improving on my attempt to get a student to stop thinking of Chinese as sharing certain linguistic features with English.

12. See Aoki Masaru, "What are 'Empty Words'?" (in Japanese), *Chugoku Bungaku Ho* IV (April, 1956), p. 98.

13. I have drawn this material from Aoki, p. 106. Other examples are given there.

14. See my *Shih Ching Rhetoric*, pp. 175-99.

15. Even proper nouns can perhaps be assigned to this class. See Chou, *Chung-kuo ku-tai yü-fa*, Vol. 1, p. 79. Cf. *Hamlet*, "It out-Herods Herod" (III, ii).

16. Cf. "If thou thou'st him thrice, it shall not be amiss," Shakespeare, *Twelfth Night* III, ii, 48.

17. See Chou Fa-kao, "Word-classes in Classical Chinese," paper read before the Ninth International Congress of Linguists, August 27-31, 1962, at Cambridge, Mass. (mimeo), p. 6.

18. René Wellek and Austin Warren, *Theory of Literature* (New York: Harcourt, Brace, 1956), 3rd ed., p. 196.

19. "Chariots rattle, rattle,/ Horses whinny, whinny./ Each marching man has bow and arrows at his waist./ Parents, wives, children, run, saying goodbye./ In the dust, you cannot see the Hsien-yang Bridge."

20. Cf. Demetrius, *On Style* (London and New York: Loeb Classical Library, 1927), with English translation by W. Rhys Roberts, 185, for examples from Plato of this kind of onomatopoeia.

21. Demetrius subdivided onomatopoeia into (1) "imitation of an experience" (*kata mimesin pathous*) and (2) "imitation of an action" (*kata mimesin pragmatos*): II, 94.

Chapter Fourteen

1. See Valéry, "Questions de Poésie," *Variété* III (Paris: Gallimard, 1936), pp. 45-46.

2. Quintilian, XX, i, 14.

3. See Phoibammon, "Concerning Schemes" (in Greek), *Rhetores Graeci*, ed. Leonard Spengel (1853), p. 45.

4. Gladys Doidge Willcock and Alice Walker, eds. *The Arte of*

English Poesie [1589], by George Puttenham (Cambridge, 1936). Cited by Sister Miriam Joseph, p. 48.

5. See Sister Miriam Joseph, p. 306.

6. Demetrius, V, 267.

7. Aristotle, *Rhetoric*, III, xii, 4.

8. Wellek and Warren, *Theory of Literature*, p. 178.

9. Kennedy notes that any of three relations may obtain between two syllables in close juncture: stress on the first syllable; stress on the second syllable; stress equally on both syllables. He symbolizes the three possibilities, as follows: (1) o·o (2) o.o (3) o:o. We might call relation (1) "adjunction," relation (2) "subjunction," and relation (3) "conjunction." (See Kennedy, "Word-classes in Classical Chinese," *Selected Works*, pp. 340 and 342.) Then the line "Tzu tzu sun sun," reading *not* tzu:tzu sun:sun but rather *tzu·tzu sun·sun*, could be translated as "sons' sons, and grandsons' grandsons." Cf. Kennedy, "A Study of the Particle *Yen*," *Selected Works*, p. 31.

10. See below, p. 136, for lines in which Juan Chi used diacope, interrupted by the line-end pause, to imitate birds' flight. Juan's effect is quite similar to this *Book of Songs* scheme, although where the *Songs* poet used other words for "glide," Juan used the line-end pause for it. Juan used epizeuxis, the *Songs* poet used diacope. I hesitate to speculate about the difference between hawks' flight and cranes' flight: such speculation is not much in fashion now.

11. Cf. Peacham, quoted by Sister Miriam Joseph on p. 339. Peacham says that the effect of paregmenon "is twofold, to delight the ear by the derived sound, and to move the mind with a consideration of the nigh affinitie and concord of the matter."

12. "Paronomastic gloss" is a translation of the Chinese term *yin-hsun*, "sound-gloss." The term "annominative gloss" would better cover the various actual forms of *yin-hsun*, because they commonly are paregmenonic. Cf. Bodman, *A Linguistic Study of the Shih Ming* (Cambridge, Mass.: Harvard University Press, 1954). Georg von der Gabelentz, *Chinesische Grammatik* (Halle, 1960), p. 524, says: "Oft, zumal in Definitionen, ist das Wortspiel zugleich ein *graphisches*, den phonetischen Schriftbestandtheil mitbetreffendes, und dannbewusst oder unbewusst—etymologisches." Some later glosses are purely graphic: they could not function in the spoken language; for example, *jen che jen ye* (" 'Humanitas' means to 'be human' "); *li yueh li* (" 'Patterns' we call [social] 'patterns.' ")

13. After the example itself and the poem number, I give the Archaic pronunciation of the cognate words as given by Bernhard Karlgren in *Word-Families in Chinese* (Stockholm, 1934). Then I shall give the Karlgren definition for the cognates. Next I shall identify the particular phonetic category, as given in *Word-Families*. Finally,

I shall identify the particular family (as listed in *Word-Families*) to which the cognates belong, so that the reader can if he wishes find out more about the etymological affiliation of the words in question. For more information on paregmenon, and on paregmenon in *The Songs*, see my *Shih Ching Rhetoric*, pp. 136-74.

Chapter Fifteen

1. *Cf.* above, p. 158, n. 13.

2. For shuai, Karlgren gives in *Grammata Serica Recensa* (Stockholm, 1957), 498, the Archaic pronunciation "sliwət." He says in *Word-Families*, "Words with initial consonant groups (kl- gl- etc.) I consider to be so risky that I have only adduced them in a few cases" (p. 58).

3. Cf. Peacham, that phonetic similarity gives "a pleasant facilitie in a Proverbe . . . as, to hold with the hare, and hunt with the hound: soone ripe, soone rotten." See Sister Miriam Joseph, p. 305.

4. See Karlgren, *Grammata Serica Recensa*, 818 and 828.

5. See Mayhew and McNaughton, *A Gold Orchid*.

6. Some editions show no stanza division here.

7. Cf. Hans Frankel, "Ts'ao Chih's Poetry: an Attempt at a New Approach," *Journal of the American Oriental Society* 84.1 (March, 1964), pp. 4-5.

8. Curtius suggests that "mannerism" replace "Romanticism" in the terminology of "literary science." See his discussion, *Europäische Literatur und Lateinisches Mittelalter*, p. 277.

9. See Liu Ta-chieh, *Chung-kuo wen-hsueh fa-chan shih* (Shanghai: Ku-tien wen-hsüeh ch'u-pan-she, 1958), 3 vols., Vol. I, p. 288.

10. One classical Occidental term is "climax." See Sister Miriam Joseph, p. 83. But a German term is *die Kette*, that is, "chain."

11. See Gabelentz, *Chinesische Grammatik*, p. 523.

12. Heinz Scharschuch says "in charakteristischster Ausprägung, Form wie Inhalt des Gedicht zugleich symbolisierend." See his "Chiasmus," *Gottfried von Strassburg: Stilmittel-Stilästhetik* (Berlin: Ebering, 1938), pp. 41-42.

13. The achievement of variety may, of course, validly be one of the artistic purposes for the achievement of which a rhetorical scheme is employed. Wang Li writes, "If the content tend at certain points to become monotonous, the poet should try for *formal* variation," *Chinese Poetics* (in Chinese) (Shanghai: Chiao-yü ch'u-pan-she, 1962), p. 182.

14. Also: "We will never negotiate out of fear, but we will never fear to negotiate." Shakespeare writes, "A sentence is but a chev'ril glove to a good wit. How quickly the wrong side may be turned

outward!" The scheme has great appeal. Many other famous quotations in this form might be adduced.

15. The *Ad Herrenium* gives the example, "A poem ought to be a painting that speaks; a painting ought to be a silent poem" (IV, xxviii, 39).

16. See Liu Ta-chieh, Vol. II, pp. 48-49. The scheme in these lines is composed of contrasted ideas of a special kind: they form an enigma, or statement which appears to contradict itself ("You have deserved nobly of your country, and you have not deserved nobly"). Sometimes this scheme is called paradox, although paradox also is used to designate a statement that is contrary to the consensus.

Chapter Sixteen

1. See my *Shih Ching Rhetoric*, pp. 200-20.

2. Ch'ü Wan-li, *Shih Ching shih-i* (Taipei: Chung-hua wen-hua ch'u-pan shih-ye wei-yuan-hui, 3 vols., 1952-53), Vol. I, p. 32, glosses like this: "ts'u yen pi nü shih wei mei li che."

Selected Bibliography

The Book of Songs probably has more exegetical literature written on it than any book in the world. I have tried to give the curious reader something to get him started. The specialist seeking a more erudite bibliography may look at my "Shih Ching Rhetoric."

PRIMARY SOURCES

CH'EN, CH'ING-LING. *Shih Ching Pai-hua I-chu.* Tainan: Piaochün Ch'u-pan-she, 1968. Amusing and sometimes delightful modern-Chinese versions of the 160 "Airs of the States."

COUVREUR, S. *Cheu King.* Hien Hien: Imprimerie de la Mission catholique, 1916. (original edition: Ho Chien Fu, 1896). Couvreur's version is useful because it is the only available translation in which the translator consistently follows the traditional Chinese interpretations.

FEDORENKO, H. T., and A. E. ADALIS. Ed. and trans. *Shi-tsin.* Moscow: Akademia Nauk, 1957. Russian version, with an essay by Fedorenko.

KARLGREN, BERNHARD. Trans. *Book of Odes.* Stockholm: Museum of Far Eastern Antiquities, 1957.

LEGGE, JAMES. Trans. *The She King.* Vol. IV in *The Chinese Classics.* 5 vols. Hong Kong: Hong Kong University Press, 1960. First published one hundred years ago, Legge's version of *The Songs* is indispensable—more because of its prolegomena and notes than because of its translations of the songs. The reader seeking more *information* about the songs should make this his first stop.

Mao-shih yin-te. Ed. by William Hung et al. Cambridge: Harvard-Yenching Institute Sinological Index Series No. 9. Reprinted, Tokyo, 1962. The Chinese texts with a very useful index (i.e., concordance).

POUND, EZRA. Trans. *The Classic Anthology.* Cambridge: Harvard University Press, 1954. See my note above, p. 151.

Shih Ching Pai-hua hsin chieh. Editorial Board of Wen-hua t'u-shu kung-szu. Taipei: Wen-hua t'u-shu kung-szu, n.d. Text and modern version of all 305 poems. Not so exciting as Ch'en Ch'ing-ling's versions (see above).

Shih-san-ching chu-shu fu chiao-k'an-chi. Shanghai: Kuo-hsüeh cheng-li she, 1935. Compendium of exegetical materials.

WALEY, ARTHUR. *The Book of Songs*. New York: Grove Press, 1960. The most accurate English translation. See my note, above, p. 151.

WANG CHING-CHIH. *Shih Ching T'ung-shih*. Taipei: Fujen Univ. Literature Division, 1968. Six hundred and sixty-seven pages of text and annotations.

YOSHIKAWA KOJIRO. *Shikyo Kokufu*. Tokyo: Iwanami, 1959. Texts with Japanese "pony," translation, notes, and discussion of the 160 "Airs of the States," by Japan's foremost authority on Chinese poetry.

SECONDARY SOURCES

Most of the books below deal with *The Book of Songs*, or with directly relevant philosophical or historical material. Some few deal in a general way with "style" in poetry.

CHOU FA-KAO. "Reduplicatives in the Book of Odes," *Bulletin of the Institute of History and Philology of Academia Sinica* XXXIV, ii (1963).

CH'Ü WAN-LI. *Shih Ching Shih-i*. Taipei: Chung-hua wen-hua ch'u-pan shih-ye wei-yuan-hui, 1952-53. Good notes on a limited number of poems.

CRUMP, JAMES I., JR. *Intrigues: Studies of the Chan-kuo Ts'e*. Ann Arbor: University of Michigan Press, 1964. Proposes a very interesting theory on style in the *Policies of War*.

CURTIUS, ERNST ROBERT. *Europäische Literatur und Lateinisches Mittelalter*. 4th ed. Bern: Francke, 1963. Curtius is not writing about Chinese literature, but no one interested in poetry, style, or modern *Weltliteratur* can afford to ignore his work. An English translation is published by Bollingen.

DEMETRIUS. *On Style;* with an English translation by W. Rhys Roberts. London and New York: Loeb Classical Library, 1927.

Hsien-Ch'in wen-hsueh shih ts'an-kao tzu-liao. Ed. Peking University Department of Chinese Literature. Peking: 1962. Texts, notes, and discussion of early literary works, including *The Book of Songs*.

HIGHTOWER, JAMES ROBERT. *Han-shih wai chuan*. Cambridge: Harvard University Press, 1952. Translation of an early Chinese "Bartlett's Quotations" based on *The Book of Songs*. Interesting and amusing, even if not relevant.

JOSEPH, SISTER MIRIAM. *Shakespeare's Use of the Arts of Language*. New York: Columbia University Press, 1949. Useful because it presents what Mark Van Doren calls "the best rhetorical theory Europe ever had." The examples are beautifully chosen.

KARLGREN, BERNHARD. *Glosses on the Book of Odes*. Stockholm: Museum of Far Eastern Antiquities, 1946. Material for textual study and analysis.

————. "Shi King Researches," *Bulletin of the Museum of Far Eastern Antiquities* IV (1932).

KENNEDY, GEORGE A. *Selected Works*. Ed. Tien-yi Li. New Haven: Far Eastern Publications, 1964. Especially relevant are the articles "Metrical 'Irregularity' in the Shih Ching," "Interpretation of the *Ch'un-Ch'iu*," "Fenollosa, Pound and the Chinese Character," and "A Note on Ode 220." But much of the other work in this volume is obliquely relevant.

LEGGE, JAMES. Trans. *The Chinese Classics*. 5 vols. Hong Kong: Hong Kong University Press, 1960. Besides *The Songs*, which are vol. IV, *The Chinese Classics* contains the standard translation of *The Analects*, *The Great Learning*, *The Unwobbling Pivot*, (all vol. I); of the *Mencius* (vol. II); of *The Book of Documents* (vol. III); and of *The Spring and Autumn Annals* and *Mr. Left's History* (vol. V).

————. Trans. *The Texts of Taoism*. New York, 1962.

LIN YUTANG. *The Wisdom of Laotse*. New York: Modern Library, 1948.

LIU TA-CHIEH. *Chung-kuo wen-hsueh fa-chan shih*. 3 vols. Shanghai: Ku-tien wen-hsueh ch'u-pan-she, 1958. Good survey of "Chinese literature, its history and its development."

LIU TSU-TSE. "Kuo Feng yü Ying-kuo tsao-ch'i shih-ko chih pi-chiao," *Proceedings of the Chinese Literature Society* of Hong Kong University, 1957-58. Comparative literature on *The Songs*, comparing "Airs of the States" to early English poetry.

LU K'AN-JU and FENG YUAN-CHÜN. *Chung-kuo shih-shih*. 3 vols. Peking: Tso-chia ch'u-pan-she, 1958.

MAYHEW, LENORE, and WILLIAM McNAUGHTON. *A Gold Orchid*. Tokyo and Rutland, Vermont: Tuttle, in production. Translations of 115 "Music Bureau Pieces," with an Introduction, Appendix, and notes. Especially useful to students of Chapter 5, above.

McNAUGHTON, WILLIAM. *Chinese Literature: an Anthology*. Tokyo and Rutland, Vermont: Tuttle (to be published). Translations of poetry, fiction, philosophy, and drama, with introductory sections on periods and genres.

————. *The Taoist Vision*. Ann Arbor: University of Michigan Press, 1971.

POUND, EZRA. *Cantos*. New York: New Directions, 1948. Cantos LII-LXI present "the Confucian idea going into action" in Chinese history.

————. Trans. *The Great Digest* and the *Unwobbling Pivot*. New York: New Directions, 1961. Pound's version of two canonic Confucian texts.

————. *Section: Rock-Drill de los cantares*. New York: New Directions, 1955. Poetry and erudite notes on the general history of China.

Shih Ching yen-chiu lun-wen chi. Ed. by Jen-min wen-hsueh ch'u-pan she pien-chi-pu. Peking: Jen-min wen-hsueh ch'u-pan she, 1959. Essays and scholarly articles on *The Songs*.

Style in Language. Ed. Thomas A. Sebeok. Cambridge, Mass.: Technology Press of M.I.T., 1966. The latest in stylistics: some, good; some, *faciunt nae intelligendo, ut nihil intelligant*.

VALÉRY, PAUL. *Aesthetics*. Trans. Ralph Manheim. New York: Pantheon, 1964.

————. *The Art of Poetry*. Trans. Denise Folliot. New York: Viking, 1958.

————. *Dossiers* I. Paris: Janin, 1946.

————. *Variété* III. Paris: Gallimard, 1936.

WALEY, ARTHUR. Trans. *The Analects*. London: Allen and Unwin, 1958.

————. *The Way and Its Power*. London: Allen and Unwin, 1934. Waley on Taoism, with translations.

WANG LI. *Han-yü shih-lü-hsueh*. Shanghai: Chiao-yü ch'u-pan she, 1962. No better work exists on "Chinese poetics."

WATSON, BURTON. *Early Chinese Literature*. New York: Columbia University Press, 1962. A "survey-type" book, beginning as early as *The Book of Songs*, running to a good deal later.

WEI CH'ING-CHIH. *Shih-jen yü-hsueh*. Shanghai: Commercial Press, 1958. Premodern discussion of his craft by a Chinese poet. The title is rather fanciful: "Jade Filings from the Poets."

Index

Alexander Nevsky, 100, 134
Aquinas, St. Thomas, 118
Aristotle, 51, 107, 127, 158
Austen, Jane, 145

Book of Documents, The, 17, 18, 19, 20, 22, 23, 30-31, 150, 163
Book of Rites, The, 28, 150
Book of Songs, The: Airs of the States, 13, 53, 92, 93, 96, 105, 145, 163; as poetry, 15-16; "ancestor worship" and, 15, 24-25, 27, 38, 42; carpe diem in, 67-69; and cheng ming, 17, 18, 80; chih (see education); Chinese empire and, 14-15; collection of, 14; Confucian values and, 13, 15; Courtly Songs, 13, 92, 105, 145; "Decade of T'ang, The," 146; education and, 20, 22-23; epithalamia in, 56-57; equity and, 20, 23-24; erotic poetry in, 51-56; Five Relations, the, and, 29-32; "Great Preface," 14, 105-6, 125; Heaven's mandate in, 17-18; humanitas in, 20-22, 23; I (see equity); jen (see humanitas); later Chinese poetry and, Preface, 79-81, 96-97, 112, 123, 137-39, 142-43, 148-49; li (see ritual and manners); "Little Preface," 106; Major Courtly Songs, 13, 14, 93, 96; Minor Courtly Songs, 13-14, 93, 95, 96; occasional poetry in, 61-67; Odes (Odes of the Temple and Altar), 13, 14, 29, 86, 91-92, 93, 96, 105, 145; organization of, 13-14; "poems of separation" and, 43-49; ritual and manners in, 20, 24-29; "sennin" in, 74; "seraglio

poetry" and, 58-60; "Songs of Cheng, The," 16, 52, 150; "Songs of Wei, The," 86; Taoism in, 72-76; Tê and, 18-20; T'ien-ming (see Heaven's mandate); war in, 33-42
Book of Songs, The, style in: allegory, 110-13; alliterative compounds (see shuang sheng); anadiplosis (see links); anaphora, 132-33; antimetabole, 142-43; chain, 138-39; chiasmus, 139-42; diacope, 128-29; diction, 13, 53, 145; distichs, 85-86, 148; epistrophe, 133-34; epizeuxis, 127-28; figures of grammar, 146-48; figures of thought, 144-46; fu, 98, 105-6; hsing, 98-106; links, 135-38; main form, 91-97; metaphor, 107-10; meter, 82-84; metonymy, 114-15, 124; onomatopoeia, 116, 123-24; paregmenon, 130-31; paronomasia, 116-23; pi, 98, 105-6; rhyme, 86-90; rhyming compounds (see tieh-yun); shuang sheng, 126; simile, 113-14; symploce, 135; synecdoche, 114; tieh-tzu, 126; tieh-yun, 126; traductio, 129-30.

Brown, Claude, 71, 153
Buck, Pearl, 33, 152
Bunting, Basil, 130

Chaucer, 73
Ch'ien Lung Emperor, 23
Chien Wen Ti (see "Peruser of Literature" Emperor)
Chin Ch'ang-hsu, 138
Chou Fa-kao, Preface, 85, 154, 157, 162